# PRAISE FOR KATIE BERRY'S "30 ORGANIZED H[...]

Katie breaks things down in logical order and helps you to see how to do things so they work for you, which may not be like your mother, friend or acquaintance's method!

— LINDA JANE, ON AMAZON

Thank you Katie Berry, this was like having a good friend over to help make things refreshing and fun!

— AL, ON AMAZON

Thank you, Katie Berry! I wish my mother had taught me how to keep house this way! (I wish someone had taught HER this way.)

— CATHERINE FROM WHIDBEY, ON AMAZON

A life-changing book. Katie's comprehensive approach worked wonders in my out-of-control home.

— NANCYB, ON AMAZON

# CLEANING 101

# CLEANING 101

*Lifesaving Habits to Rescue Your Home*

## KATIE BERRY

All rights reserved. No portion of this book may be reproduced in any form, including information storage and retrieval or LLM training, without written permission from the publisher or author, except by a reviewer who may quote brief passages in a review or as permitted by U.S. copyright law. This includes illustrations and recipes.

First paperback edition June 2024.

ISBN-13: 979-8-9910031-0-0 (paperback)

ISBN-13: 979-8-9910031-1-7 (ebook)

Published by KTB Creative, LLC

# DEDICATION

*To Tate.*

*Thank you for always believing in me.*

*Love,*
*Mom*

# CONTENTS

| | |
|---|---|
| Acknowledgements | xi |
| Introduction | xiii |

### Part One
### CLASS OVERVIEW

| | |
|---|---|
| 1. Study Habits | 3 |
| 2. Doing is Being | 5 |
| 3. What's In Your Way? | 8 |
| 4. Crib Notes | 16 |
| 5. Absence Policy | 22 |

### Part Two
### PREREQUISITES

| | |
|---|---|
| 6. Ease Into It | 29 |
| 7. Self-Sabotage | 31 |

### Part Three
### A BRIEF PRIMER ON CLEANING PRACTICES

| | |
|---|---|
| 8. Dealing with Dust | 35 |
| 9. Styles of Surface Cleaning | 37 |
| 10. Putting a Polish on It | 40 |
| 11. Vacuuming Secrets | 43 |
| 12. Mopping Matters | 46 |
| 13. What's In My Cleaning Closet? | 49 |

### Part Four
### THE ASSIGNMENTS

| | |
|---|---|
| 14. Kitchen Cleaning 101 | 57 |
| 15. Living Spaces Cleaning 101 | 67 |
| 16. Bedroom Cleaning 101 | 79 |
| 17. Bathroom Cleaning 101 | 87 |
| 18. Entryway 101 | 95 |
| 19. Home Office 101 | 100 |

### Part Five
# RESEARCH LAB

| | |
|---|---|
| 20. My Weekly Routine | 107 |
| 21. How I Manage it with ADHD | 112 |
| 22. Getting the Family Involved | 114 |
| 23. Take the Plunge | 120 |
|     Also by Katie Berry | 124 |

# ACKNOWLEDGEMENTS

No work is ever really done alone, even when it feels otherwise. So, I want to thank Rachel Slaikawitz and Laura Gerlach for not only reading this over, but for reading me well. I am so grateful that you gave me the room to grow and discover myself without treating that need as a bridge on fire. Your patient friendship reminds me of the woman I want to become. Thank you.

For fourteen years, I've sat at a computer doing all the things needed to write and maintain HousewifeHowTos.com and its social media channels. But even when I've been the only person at the desk, I've never been alone.

The wonderful thing about my job is how it brings me together with women all over the world, from Whitehorse to Whakatāne and San Francisco to Shrivardhan. I am honored and grateful that you've allowed me to be part of your lives and have taken my words as guidance. You've been part of my life, too, and I love the community we've shared.

Most of all, I thank **you** for your patience. It's been ten years since I published my first cleaning book. Over 45,000 copies later, I wanted to make sure I had something new to say before I published another.

I hope you find it worth the wait.

# INTRODUCTION

I have never tried to put lipstick on a pig, but I imagine it's not an easy thing to do. I'm far from tiny or frail, but even if I held the pig still, it would just rub off the lipstick immediately. But what if I went about it differently?

What if I fed the pig some foods that stained its lips? A handful of pomegranate seeds would add a little red. Strawberries would add even more. Beets? Now we're talking! Feeding those to the pig consistently, before the color had a chance to fade, would accomplish the same thing without all the struggles.

So, which would you choose: the hard way that achieves temporary results, or an easy route that produces long-lasting ones? It seems like an obvious choice and yet when it comes to cleaning our homes, so many people do it the hard way.

This book is for people who'd rather not wrestle a pig. It's for those willing to learn how smaller, consistent daily efforts add up to an enormous win. Most of all it's for people who'd rather not spend time in a pigsty, especially if there's a low-effort way out. There is, and I'm excited to share it with you.

So welcome to a basic approach to care for your home without

## INTRODUCTION

making a career of it. If you're an old hand at cleaning, some of the info that follows will feel like a refresher course. Use it to confirm your knowledge and boost your confidence that you've been doing things right all along. But if you're new to cleaning, or if you've been struggling, you'll find practical help in these pages.

*This book is for people who'd rather not wrestle a pig.*

Treat this as you would any introductory book: start at the beginning and continue through to the end, because each section builds on the previous one. If you jump around, you'll likely get lost and overwhelmed. Trust that I put things in this order for a reason, and your patience will pay off with a system to keep your home under control for the rest of your life.

Ready? Then take your seat and let's get started with Cleaning 101.

## Part One
# CLASS OVERVIEW

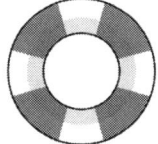

Before we dive into things, let's talk a little about what to expect. You see, we won't be cleaning your home top to bottom right away. If you think that means you're in the wrong place, let me explain.

Jumping into the deep end untrained is a recipe for drowning. I want to help you never need another cleaning book or chore chart again. My goal is to rescue your weekends as well as your vacations by sharing simple, consistent routines that will keep your head above water no matter how busy life gets.

*Chapter One*
# STUDY HABITS

I've been helping people learn to manage their homes for almost 14 years. Yet three times a year, without fail, my website traffic and book sales soar: the first week of January, the week before Easter, and the week after Labor Day.

Why then?

Because that's when people who have made New Year's Resolutions or who are deep cleaning for Spring or Fall realize it's an enormous effort. So it dawns on them, they'd rather just get their homes under control *once and for all*.

And every year as my Inbox and DMs blow up, I sound like a broken record repeating there's no way to get your home clean "once and for all" unless you move out and wrap the place in cling film. Even then, dust would find a way. You might as well spend the entire weekend brushing your teeth so they're clean *once and for all*.

Just as going on a toothbrushing binge won't have lasting results, binge cleaning won't produce a consistently clean home, either.

Cleaning is a process, not a project. It's a skill you develop by repeating a routine until it becomes a habit. And habits are shorthand for describing what matters to you.

Want a clean home? Then you need to get in the habit of cleaning it. It's that easy, and that hard. But aren't most habits? And once you fall out of a habit, getting back into the swim of things can feel like you're starting all over again.

Because you are.

## Chapter Two
# DOING IS BEING

Last fall, I watched the movie *Nyad*. At age 60, Dianna Nyad decided to once again try swimming the Florida Straits, an unfulfilled goal from her youth. Her determination and grit profoundly inspired me.

As we get older, it often feels like life's great adventures and changes are behind us. Sometimes, it even feels like society expects us at a certain age to sit in our rockers, take up our darning, and slowly fade into gray. I don't think it has to be like that. I don't *want* it to be like that.

I'd just turned 56 when I saw the movie and realized it had been almost 40 years since I'd been in a pool. But once upon a time, I'd been such an avid swimmer that I'd practice every weekday and compete in meets on Saturday. On Sundays, I just swam for the fun of it. I loved everything about swimming and had a wall of trophies and ribbons to show for it.

Then one day, a casual insult from someone I admired took all the joy out of it. So, I quit. Forty years later, I'd heard enough interviews of this person to know they often said appalling things.

I'd let one nasty comment from a jerk take away something I loved, but it was time for that to change. I wanted to be a swimmer again.

Our local outdoor pools had already closed for the season, so I figured my plan would have to wait until later. Then I heard someone mention swimming at the community center's indoor pool. I took it as a sign and promised myself I'd go to the very next session, which turned out to be at 6 AM the following morning.

As someone who is not, never has been, and never will be a morning person, I nearly backed out. Then I realized that at that hour, I'd probably have the pool to myself—perfect for an introvert who hadn't swum a lap in decades.

My first minutes in the water, it was like the years had washed away and I was a kid again. I felt buoyant and literally was: *fat floats*. Four decades of sedentary living had done some serious damage. Swimming just one lap left me gasping for air and praying not to vomit. I dog-paddled to the side, waited for the nausea to pass, and went home.

I'd proven to myself I could still swim, and that meant I could get around to doing it any time I wanted. Maybe I should lift weights for a or get back on the treadmill to get in shape first? Maybe I should wait until New Year's and do it as a Resolution? Sounds silly, right — why not just swim?

But that's exactly what people do with cleaning. Either they'll put it off until they take care of a few other things, or they'll plunge into it and clean their homes top to bottom and wind up exhausted. Either way, their homes get messy again because they didn't pick up the habit of keeping things tidy.

It's the consistency, the day-to-day showing up and putting in effort that makes all the difference. For swimmers, it's consistently swimming laps. For people with clean homes, it's consistently cleaning.

- They don't think of it as having to earn their rest, they think of it as part of living.
- They don't do it so they can feel good about doing other things. They do it because they like the results.
- They don't feel like they're missing out on fun. They see it as fulfilling a goal each time they put in the work.
- It's not something they do to prove anything to anyone, or to make anyone else happy. They do it for themselves.

*Habits are shorthand for describing what matters to you.*

To be a swimmer, I must swim. No one can do it for me. To have a clean home, someone needs to clean it.

Does that someone need to be you? Not necessarily. If you've got enough money to hire someone to clean your home, hand this book to your housekeeper and go get a pedicure. For the rest of us, having a clean house means we have to put time and effort into it.

I wish it were otherwise, because I would write that book for you! And then I'd be so rich that I'd have a home with a massive indoor pool and people who cleaned it all for me.

Hey, a girl can dream, right?

## Chapter Three
# WHAT'S IN YOUR WAY?

Friction occurs when things work against each other, causing wear and tear. Think of sandpaper on wood: the bumps smooth out, but the sandpaper loses its grit. The brakes on your car use friction to stop the wheels, and over time, they wear out too. Drag your hips in the water when you're swimming, and your body creates friction that slows you down and wears you out.

You encounter friction when cleaning, too. Sometimes it's physical, like scrubbing a surface. Other times, it's mental, like not having enough time or interest. And when you're stressed or overwhelmed, that lack of interest can turn into active avoidance.

If you're struggling to find motivation to clean, it's almost always due to psychological friction. Something is making it feel like a pointless hassle. That can look different for each of us.

- Anxiety about what others think or expect.
- The inconvenience of just getting started.
- Feeling rushed or short on time.
- Physical limitations like illness or aging.

- Believing that it's not worth it if you can't do it perfectly.

Ultimately, these are all mental obstacles. Every one of us has our own obstacles that'll sap our motivation, including me. But let's plan a route around them by looking at each one in turn.

## ANXIETY ABOUT EXPECTATIONS

Gym anxiety nearly kept me from swimming again, even after I'd gotten back into it for a while. I'm older, I'm fat, and I've got psoriatic arthritis which leads to horribly swollen joints. So, every morning, I'd lie in bed imagining someone was thinking mean things about me or, worse, saying them out loud.

As with most of my anxieties, there was no recent basis for that fear: everyone I encountered had been supportive and encouraging. So where was this coming from?

The answer was in the past. Specifically, the day our swim coach invited a former Olympic swimmer to provide individual feedback to help us improve. In front of the entire co-ed team, this celebrity explained that my fat rear-end kept my hips from dragging in the water, like a buoy, which helped me swim faster.

Being a teenage girl, I was excruciatingly embarrassed having the size of my bottom discussed publicly like that, but back then we had to put up with such things.

Something else I had to put up with? Being called "Buoy Butt" for days. Later that week, the coach announced I was swimming last in the relay at the next meet. "Buoy Butt can bring up the rear!" he chuckled. But I didn't. I went home from practice in tears and never went back.

Hurtful memories about cleaning can trigger similar feelings. We call it *cleaning anxiety* if it's a mild nervousness, and *cleaning trauma* if it has a more profound effect. Maybe you had a parent who always found fault with the way you cleaned things or used cleaning as a form of punishment? Maybe you were taunted for having a messy room or made to feel inferior because you didn't clean the way someone thought you should?

Those memories are always with us, but they don't have to control what we do today.

That Olympian swimmer probably wouldn't remember making that comment. Who knows, he might even apologize. Likewise, the parents who criticized how you did things, or who used chores to punish you, may not have realized you'd carry that around long-term. Even if they wouldn't apologize, they don't have power over you anymore now that you're an adult.

My friend, as an adult it's clean when *you* say it is. There's nothing to be anxious about. You're not cleaning your home because you did something wrong. You're cleaning because you deserve a home that's comforting, not chaotic.

Think of cleaning as a gift to your future self. When you see areas you've cleaned, thank your past self for that gift. Literally out loud. Doing this acts as counter-friction, wearing down that psychological obstacle until it no longer stands in the way of having the clean home you deserve.

## INCONVENIENCES

Pushing past a small inconvenience can make you feel proud of yourself. What determination! What moxie! Look at you go!

But dealing with one after another can wear you down. Imagine how you'd feel trying to climb a series of steps that are each half as tall as you:

One: *Um, okay.*
Two: *Well, that's a bit of effort.*
Three: *You know, I'm getting kind of tired.*
Four: *Seriously???*
Five: **NOPE.**

When inconveniences mount up, they can stop you in your tracks. So, think about the type of things that repeatedly make cleaning a hassle, and plan around them. Here are some common examples:

**Problem:** You're out of cleaning product.
**Solution:** Learn what household ingredients can act as substitutes, so you don't have to stop.

**Problem:** Some cleaning tasks are painful or feel dangerous due to physical limitations or aging.
**Solution:** Switch to adaptive cleaning tools that are lightweight and easier to use.

**Problem:** You get worn out carrying things up and downstairs.
**Solution:** Have a cleaning caddy with basic supplies under each sink, and a separate vacuum on each level of your home.

**Problem:** There's too much stuff in the way.
**Solution:** Make storage more convenient and spend 5 minutes a day just putting things away.

**Problem:** You don't have a lot of time to clean.
**Solution:** Keep reading. I got you.

Of course, other things can sap your motivation to clean, too, like family members leaving their stuff around or just not being in the mood. I'll address those later.

For now, focus on noticing when cleaning starts to feel like a hassle. Then, put your brain to work coming up with ways to prevent that. The more you anticipate and eliminate friction, the easier it will be to stick to a cleaning routine.

*When you repeatedly encounter the same obstacle, ask yourself what would make that step frictionless.*

## WORK WITH YOUR INNER CLOCK

Have I mentioned that I'm not a morning person? When I started swimming again, the 6 AM lap times became a struggle, especially as the seasons changed. It was an excuse waiting to happen, and I felt the friction starting to build.

At first, I looked at the other lap times, but they were during my work hours so I'd have to rearrange my day. That would've solved one source of friction (the early hour) but introduced another (inconvenience).

When your inner clock is the obstacle, you'll have a better chance of success by changing when you clean, rather than trying to change yourself. For me, that meant switching to a gym where the pool is open for laps 18 hours a day. It's more expensive, but also more realistic.

**Not a morning person?** Don't buy into the "wake 30

minutes earlier" nonsense. You'll spend 30 minutes trying to clear your head and end up angry with yourself, so what's the point?

**Wiped out after work?** Try the morning approach. With good habit chains and daily tidying, you only need a spare 20-30 minutes.

**Not a morning, afternoon, or evening person?** I have some bad news: you need to pick one. If you can figure out a way to have a clean home without choosing, let me know when your book comes out. Seriously, I'll buy it!

## ADAPT AS NEEDED

It's been a minute since I mentioned swimming, hasn't it? Listen, it may seem like I keep coming back to that topic which has nothing to do with cleaning, but there's a reason: it has *plenty* to do with cleaning! They're both skills you can turn into a habit, and they both feel like work *even when* you like the result.

Something else they have in common: how you do them changes as you get older. The day I realized I had to stop swimming the butterfly stroke was a hard one. In my youth, that was my best event, but arthritis rules it out now. It hurt my pride admitting that, but adapting kept me swimming.

Cleaning can require adaptive changes too, especially as we get older or deal with injuries.

- If your equipment is hard to maneuver, consider lighter cleaning tools or automated, robot vacuums.
- If your grip isn't what it used to be, look for cleaning gear with rounded, padded handles. They're easier to hold and use.
- If you can't comfortably clean for longer periods, divide it into small sessions throughout the day. Even 5 minutes can work a lot of change.

When you make cleaning more physically comfortable, you'll find it's less exhausting and that means you'll dread it less, too.

## FOCUS ON THE REAL GOAL

Have you ever been to an event where someone shows up way overdressed, like wearing a skirt and heels to a picnic or a 3-piece suit to a PTA meeting? It's awkward, right? You know they're trying hard, but it seems so over the top that you can't help but wonder who they're trying to impress.

People who stress about keeping their homes spotless all the time are a bit like that. I'll let you in on a little secret: I've been both the overdressed person and the one obsessed with a clean home. Why? Because I thought people would respect me for it, but it had the opposite effect.

By trying to impress others, I made their opinions of me more important than my own. Besides being a recipe for anxiety, when people sense you're trying to impress them, they actually look down on you.

So, before you read any further, make sure you're doing it for the right reasons: to create a comfortable home that's clean enough to be healthy.

This doesn't require perfection, and it doesn't require nonstop effort, but it does require *consistency*. To help with that, identify the friction that usually stops you from cleaning consistently and plan ways to overcome it.

*Chapter Four*

# CRIB NOTES

Have you ever seen a buoy in the water? It's there to guide you around dangers. Buoys have wide bases to provide stability, so they don't tip over or go under when the winds blow or waves crash. If you've felt like you are flailing or going under while trying to keep your home clean, the routines which follow can act as a buoy.

We'll start by laying the base of habit chains and daily tidying to keep you on an even keel, even when the going gets rough. These support the weekly cleaning so it's easier and faster to do, which rescues your weekends. Then, to cap things off, the monthly tasks eliminate the need for Spring Cleaning so you can take back your vacation time, too.

## LINKING THINGS CREATES HABITS

I wasn't diagnosed with ADHD until I was 50. Before that, many things in life that seemed to come naturally to others were a struggle for me — and vice versa. I can focus intently on something

I'm interested in, which benefited me greatly as an attorney. But paying attention to boring things is *excruciating*.

The only way for me to handle mundane tasks like cleaning is to make them so automatic that I don't need to think about what I'm doing. Then, I can entertain my brain with podcasts or music, or as my husband used to put it, "just thinking big thoughts."

But having ADHD makes developing good habits a challenge. I pick up bad ones faster than ink can dry, but good habits take a lot of willpower and visual cues until they sink in.

When I left the practice of law to become a stay-at-home mom, I had to consciously cultivate good habits to run our home. At first, I created checklists like the free ones on my website. They helped me train myself and make tasks automatic. Then I kept repeating the checklists from start to finish until they were so habitual I didn't have to think about what I was doing. I just cleaned.

Checklists often fail because people treat them like recipes, swapping tasks based on their mood or skipping steps to save time. That's not their purpose. Checklists are meant to be followed in order, from start to finish, without deviation. Over time, they help you develop a routine where one action automatically follows another. Once that happens, you won't need to remember what comes next, and cleaning becomes an automatic process.

Before you laugh and toss the book aside, you should know that you're already doing this!

Imagine yourself at the bathroom sink with your toothbrush in one hand. What are you going to do next? You'll either add toothpaste or you'll get the toothbrush wet, depending on your preference, and then you'll move onto the other.

That's how a habit chain works. This system simply expands your cleaning habits to include your home.

## THE TWO-MINUTE METHOD ALTERNATIVE

While cleaning checklists are excellent tools for creating habits to clean up messes, they don't necessarily teach you to avoid making them. I didn't realize this at first. I thought if I could just make a comprehensive checklist, nothing would ever get messy again.

For the first month, I kept revising my checklists to add more details. Found the baby bag on the floor near the door? Add "Hang up baby bag!" to the checklist. Junk mail piling up on the counter? Add "Take junk mail to home office and shred it" to my list. After a while, the list was over a dozen pages long and I rarely made it all the way through.

Part of the problem is that by adding new tasks daily, I never really followed a routine. How could I develop a habit when no two days were the same?

But also, I found myself leaving things undone until I got to them on the list. For quick tasks like getting the used bottle out of the baby bag or handling junk mail, that made no sense. Grabbing the baby bottle took seconds. Once I put a shredder in the kitchen, dealing with the junk mail took just seconds, too. But looking these tasks up on the list, doing them, then checking them off took twice as long. So, all I needed to do was pay better attention.

Now, I don't know if you have ADHD or know anyone who does, but *paying better attention* isn't an option for us. Our brains don't work that way. Trying to remember every little thing we're supposed to do and when we're supposed to do it, just to avoid annoying or disappointing others, is a major source of stress, anxiety, and self-loathing.

This process, known as masking, requires constant effort. Imagine trying to always maintain perfect posture, knowing that every slip means someone gets upset with you. Exhausting doesn't begin to describe it—you might even give up at some point.

But setting reminders to stop and notice things? That's something we can work on, and that's how I started.

I realized that if I kept adding little tasks to my checklist, I was doomed. But if I found a way to prevent little messes, I'd be giving my future self less work and less stress.

Looking back, I was treating my ADHD as a source of friction and finding a way around it. At first, that way was through practicing intentional mindfulness. I did this by setting a timer for 2 minutes and cleaning or tidying everything I could before the timer went off.

Anything that could be done in two minutes was fair game, but keeping it to just two minutes was crucial. Tasks shorter than that wouldn't make a noticeable difference. But any longer, and I'd do something ADHD-inspired like completely emptying the closet to reorganize it, then stopping halfway togo read a book instead.

So, doing multiple 2-minute tidying sessions was fine, but none could be longer than 2 minutes. And no quitting until the timer went off.

*If I found a way to prevent little messes, I'd be giving my future self less work.*

Eventually, I replaced this practice with habit chains in each room, as I'll explain later. But I wanted to share this two-minute approach first, so you know there's no need to stress over habit chains if they don't work for you. Using the two-minute method once or twice a day can accomplish the same thing without masking or forcing your brain to follow a system that doesn't suit it.

Just remember, whatever approach you take will only work if you're consistent. So, let's discuss what to do if illness or other events cause waves in your routine.

## *Chapter Five*
# ABSENCE POLICY

Every week, I hear from people trying to keep their homes clean while dealing with physical or mental health conditions.

So naturally, I tell them that if they can't commit 100% to cleaning every day, regardless of how they're feeling or what they're going through, they might as well not bother, right?

*Of course, I don't say that!*

Imagine I came to you for advice after dropping out of a meditation challenge due to a migraine or asked if I should still aim for 10,000 steps even though my arthritis was flaring up. You'd be concerned that I wasn't seeing the bigger picture, right?

You'd probably tell me there's nothing to feel guilty about and that taking care of myself should be the top priority. Then, you'd advise me to ease back into things when I felt ready, instead of trying to make up for lost time, to avoid a setback. Most importantly, you'd remind me to be kind to myself. Why is it so easy to be gracious to others but not to ourselves??

Friend, I want you to cut yourself some slack. If you're dealing with a condition that limits your energy or motivation, if you're busy caring for others, or if life deals you a blow that knocks you off course, give yourself the same grace you would give to anyone you respect and admire.

It doesn't matter if that's a physical or mental condition: they both involve your health. It doesn't matter if it's short or long-term: your pain and exhaustion don't become any less real the longer you live with them. Get the rest you need, be gentle with yourself, and when you feel stronger, pick up where you left off.

And if anyone, including *yourself*, has a problem with that, remind them that the cleanliness of your home doesn't reflect your worth. It doesn't make you a better person, more competent, or more deserving of love. It just means you spent time cleaning. But if life has knocked you around, maybe having a clean home shouldn't be the biggest priority.

*When you're dealing with a health issue or other life event, the smart thing to do is to take care of yourself.*

## MAKE-UP PLAN

If that approach feels too vague, or you're not confident you'll be able to get back on track, here's a more detailed make-up plan.

> **If it's only been a day or two**, forget about what you've missed. Start with whatever you'd ordinarily be doing that day. You'll get the messy areas again next week, so relax.

> **If it's been a week or two**, forget about what you've missed. Start with whatever you'd ordinarily be doing that day. Then, for the next few days, put in a little extra effort on the daily tidying.

**If it's been a month or longer**, treat it as a fresh start and follow the plan laid out later in this book. (Please don't skip ahead to see it: you'll sabotage your success. Trust the process!)

## WHEN IT'S A PATTERN

What if you keep getting derailed at the same point? That may be a sign something deeper is going on, like *cleaning anxiety*. Before you jump back into your routine, spend some time identifying what triggered the disruption. Treat that trigger as a powerful source of psychological friction and plan how to manage or avoid it.

Maybe you need to break down a task you despise into smaller steps to make it more bearable. Or maybe you can ask a family member or friend to take it over. Even just talking to someone about what's bothering you can help by getting the negative memory out of your head so you gain a new perspective.

If the issue persists, consider that you might be dealing with something deeper known as *cleaning trauma*. This is actual emotional distress stemming from negative experiences related to cleaning tasks. It often happens when cleaning was used as a punishment in childhood, or if you faced harsh criticism or overwhelming expectations from a perfectionist parent.

Unresolved cleaning trauma can cause a negative feedback loop that keeps you from cleaning all or part of your home. Then, because it's not clean, you feel even greater distress.

But your home should be a place where you feel the safest. So, rather than letting cleaning trauma ruin that sense of safety, consider talking to a therapist to get strategies and support to work through the cause. I promise, you are not the only one to experience that kind of pain, and you deserve a life free of it.

But friend, no matter what disrupts your routine, *do not punish*

## CLEANING 101

*yourself for needing time off.* It's only cleaning. Your health and happiness matter so much more.

*Part Two*

# PREREQUISITES

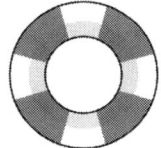

An unfortunately common approach to teaching kids how to swim involves throwing them into the deep end and counting on them to figure it out.

When my parents did that, I nearly drowned. It was years before I was brave enough to try again, and I begged for lessons rather than trust them. Fool me once, etc.

So, rather than throw you into the deep end of cleaning, let's go over a couple of things starting with the importance of easing your way in.

## *Chapter Six*
## EASE INTO IT

When you finally decide you're ready, it's tempting to dive right in. That's what I did when I switched to the gym's pool and no longer had to be up at 6 AM. After a few days of catching up on sleep, I felt stronger and less winded at the end of every session. Naturally, I decided to double the number of laps I was doing and go every weekday instead of three times a week. Brilliant, right?

Yeah, not so much. I woke up the second day in agony. On the third day, I had to ask my son to hold my toothbrush while I moved my head because I couldn't even lift the thing. I didn't make it to the pool on the fourth day, or at any point the following week. I was too sore to do much besides stay on the sofa watching TV.

Almost a week later, I was only three seasons into a 20-season show on Netflix and the sofa had started to sag in all the right places. Swimming seemed like such a silly waste of time. It's not like I planned to ever compete again, so what was the point? When I was finally able to move without pain, my first instinct wasn't to head to the pool but to the store for some ice cream.

Fortunately, God decided I didn't need that ice cream as much as a good lesson. So, I arrived at the store and realized I'd grabbed my gym bag instead of my purse. Message received: to the gym I went.

But this time, I stopped swimming when I felt tired and called it good enough. Two days later, I did the same thing. I kept that up for a week before deciding I was ready for more.

The "more" came in the form of getting advice from an expert so I could make progress without overdoing things. I found a swim coach, and now I follow a training routine that guides me to leveling up when I'm ready.

And as a Cleaning Expert, I've created this program to help you learn a new sustainable routine and make weekly progress, too. We're going to do that by forming habit chains to keep each room tidy and do daily resets that cut down how much time it takes to clean things each week. At the end, I put it all together in a schedule that eases you into the routine without overworking or exhausting you. No drowning here!

But please don't skip ahead. It won't help. In fact, you'll probably sink.

*Chapter Seven*

# SELF-SABOTAGE

Welcome back to those who skipped ahead and now feel overwhelmed! I warned you, didn't I? Which reaction did you have: *"I can't do that!"* or *"This makes no sense!"*

Listen, lots of times in life things look difficult or incomprehensible at first. But you've accomplished the "impossible" many times in your life through time and practice. Maybe you struggled with addition or subtraction in first grade, but I bet you don't count on your fingers now. Math is a skill, and the more you use it, the more automatic it becomes.

Driving? We all start off white knuckling the wheel and breaking a sweat trying to remember everything. Then it becomes so ingrained we can drive, drink coffee, hold a conversation, and sing along with the radio all at the same time. Your job, bowling, doing your hair, using a computer program—it can all feel strange and overwhelming at first, but consistent practice turns it into a familiar skill.

Cleaning is a skill too. When you do it methodically and consistently, it becomes a routine. Like adding 1+1, it becomes so automatic and simple you'll wonder how you ever struggled.

The key is not to sabotage yourself. That means taking the time to read this book from beginning to end *before you start cleaning*. That way, you'll understand how the habit chains and daily tidying take care of most messes, making weekly cleaning faster and even allowing for deep-cleaning tasks—all in less time than you're used to.

Since I'm not the only one who likes to think of herself as an exception to any rule, let me repeat this: **the best way to develop a new routine is by easing into it.** If you want a system that sticks, it's a process:

1. Learn what and how to do things.
2. Learn how often.
3. Put it into practice.

So, turn the page and let's get learning.

*Part Three*

# A BRIEF PRIMER ON CLEANING PRACTICES

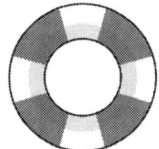

What some call "cleaning" is just shifting dirt and germs around, not actually getting rid of them. If it feels like you spend a lot of time at it, but things never feel quite clean, or if your home is looking grubbier with each passing day, it's time to brush up on your techniques.

I tried to think of ways to make this part interesting, but it's *cleaning*. Unless I write it as a rhyming poem or draw it as a cartoon — neither of which I'm good at — there's no way to make it fun. However, that doesn't mean it's not important to know. Because what follows are my best tips to make the actual cleaning process more effective so it takes less time (even if it's still a bit dull).

*Chapter Eight*
# DEALING WITH DUST

*D*ust is an unavoidable part of life, and everything around us becomes part of it: dirt, skin flakes and hair from us or our pets, textile fibers, dried-out plant leaves, peeling paint, even the crumbs from this morning's toast. If you burn candles or vape indoors, you're adding particles to your home's air which turn into dust, too.

Since dust is lightweight, it floats around in the air then settles, and not just on tables or shelves — though that's where we most often notice it. Dust builds up on ceilings and walls as well as sofas, beds, lampshades, and curtains. And, of course, dust lands on our floors.

To dust well, you need to be like dust. I don't mean flakey, I mean clean in the order it falls: ceiling, walls, window and door trim, doors, shelves, sofas and chairs, tables, baseboards and finally, floors. As you dust, clean everything on each surface: ceiling fans, artwork on walls, books, decorative items on tables, and so on.

*To dust well, clean in the order it falls.*

You don't have to clean all the surfaces in a room at once. Most of us don't have that kind of time or energy. But when you're cleaning, remember that any dust you stir up will fall on lower surfaces.

So, start with the highest ones and work your way down. Use a damp cloth and rinse it often. Finally, clean the floor to get rid of any particles that settled. Boom, now you're not just moving the dust around, you're getting it out of your home.

*Chapter Nine*
# STYLES OF SURFACE CLEANING

*P*eople often think things are worn out, permanently stained or too grubby to keep because they don't know how to clean them properly. That's why I used to cruise garage sales for things I knew would fetch a good price on eBay after a little glow-up. One carved wooden box needed just a few minutes of cleaning and oiling. After that, it sold for fifty times what I'd paid—not bad for 5 minutes of work!

The same principle applies to homes. If you've ever sold a home, you know Realtors harp about cleaning and decluttering — and for good reason. A clean home fetches a higher price, just like that wooden box. But even if you're not planning to sell, cleaning the surfaces of your home properly keeps everything from furniture to flooring looking new longer, and that protects your investment.

On the other hand, improper cleaning — like scouring a delicate surface or rubbing a stain to remove it instead of blotting — can cause permanent damage that no one, including a professional, can fix. So, let's go over the basic techniques of surface cleaning to make sure you've got this down pat.

## BLOTTING

Blotting means pressing a cloth onto a fresh stain or spill, lifting it, folding to a clean section, and pressing it down again. I imagine Elle Woods from *Legally Blonde* doing the bend and snap routine, but for me, it's "press...and *lift!*"

The goal is to transfer the mess from the surface to your cloth without spreading it. Use a white or undyed cloth to avoid color transfer and so you can see the mess being absorbed.

## WIPING

Wiping is the most common cleaning method. It involves a simple back-and-forth motion with a dry or damp cloth. Yes, I know this seems obvious, but you won't believe how many people wipe when they need to scrub, then bark at me because the mess didn't budge.

## SCRUBBING

Scrubbing is not the same thing as wiping: it uses a circular or figure 8 motion, so you're going at the grime from all directions. Textured and bumpy surfaces almost always need scrubbing to get the dirt out of all the different nooks and crannies.

Common scrubbing materials include microfiber cloths, nylon or Dobie pads, or cellulose or natural sponges. Not all are appropriate for every surface so read the labels.

## SCOURING

Scouring is a scrubbing method that uses an abrasive product or material. Baking soda, "The Pink Stuff" paste, and "Bar Keeper's Friend" are all effective products that are gentle enough for most surfaces. Melamine sponges (like "Magic Erasers") and steel wool are abrasive materials.

The biggest mistake people make when scouring is using too much water, so then things don't rub, they slide. Scouring powders or creams aren't soap: you need a barely damp surface and a barely damp cloth. Rubbing the abrasive product between these two things is what scours the surface. Be sure to rinse thoroughly when you're done to keep the product from drying on the surface — then it's a booger to clean.

## BUFFING

Buffing looks like scrubbing but it uses a clean, dry cloth on a recently cleaned surface. Working in circles removes haze and excess product. Using long, straight strokes following the grain on wood or stainless steel creates heat which can help polishes bond to the surface and look glossier.

## Chapter Ten
# PUTTING A POLISH ON IT

Routine cleaning doesn't usually involve polishing furniture, but it's nice for special occasions. Some glass surfaces need a weekly polish to look their best, too.

## WOOD

While in Europe, I went to a party at a 16th century Italian villa famed for its wooden ceilings that had been hand-polished over the centuries using linseed oil.

The dashing owner explained it's such a labor-intensive process that polishing happened somewhere in the villa every day except Christmas. Much to his embarrassment, it was his bedroom's turn that week. Now, I'm not suggesting you use linseed oil to polish wood because, as I discovered, when it's fresh it has a smell you'll never forget.

You can make your own furniture spray using a neutral oil like grapeseed, olive, or jojoba shaken with an equal amount of white vinegar, plus a couple drops of lemon essential oil if you want it to smell nice. Apply the mixture with a soft cloth in long, smooth strokes following the wood's grain, then buff with a fresh, dry cloth to create a glossy shine.

For commercial polishes, I prefer Scott's Liquid Gold because it is oil-based. Most spray polishes like Pledge and Endust use silicone-based ingredients. These create a smooth layer but can also trap dust and humidity, leading to a dull, sticky buildup over time. Oil-based polishes don't do that.

## GLASS

Many glass polishes also clean, but it's sometimes best to treat them as separate steps. For instance, glass tabletops often get grimy from fingerprints and food spills, just like outdoor glass surfaces and car windows. You'll get better results if you first clean the surface, then switch to a dry cloth and apply the polish. For mirrors and windows, buffing after polishing leaves them sparkling.

As for products, I mostly use equal parts water and white vinegar indoors. For very grimy glass indoors or out, I opt for an equal mixture of water, rubbing alcohol, and white vinegar.

If you prefer store-bought glass cleaners, I recommend alcohol-based Sprayway Glass Cleaner over Windex, which contains ammonia. Sprayway is less corrosive and it foams, so you don't wind up with a runny mess.

## METALS AND NATURAL STONE

The polishing products for metal and stone surfaces are meant to be used on a clean surface. They contain fine abrasives that gently smooth the surface so it reflects light. It's crucial to follow the product directions exactly, or you may wind up with permanent damage.

For light polishing, you can safely buff stone surfaces with baking soda or powdered white chalk and then brush or vacuum away the excess.

## Chapter Eleven
# VACUUMING SECRETS

Your vacuum isn't just for cleaning floors: it's one of the best ways to get dust out of your home, too. The key is starting with the attachments to clean soft furnishings and around the edges. Then, use your vacuum at the right setting and speed to clean the floor.

## USE THE ATTACHMENTS

When you're vacuuming a room's soft furnishings, start with the highest point and work your way down. So, vacuum the curtains first then the lampshades, sofas and chairs, and throw pillows. (Relax, I don't mean every time you clean. We'll get to the routines in a bit!)

- **Brush attachment:** The soft bristles on the brush attachment makes it perfect for cleaning curtains or dusting intricate furniture.
- **Upholstery attachments**: This attachment is small and

flat with a felt strip to lift pet hair and lint from sofas, chairs, and throw pillows.
- **Crevice tool**: The long, skinny attachment has an angled end. That angle helps it pull dust from tight spots like between sofa cushions and where walls or heavy furniture meet the floor.
- **Floor attachment:** The floor attachment that goes on the end of an upright vacuum's hose or tube is designed to get under furniture like sofas and beds.

## SWITCH FLOOR SETTINGS

Once you've finished using the attachments, adjust your vacuum so it's ready to clean the floor. This varies between models, but the idea is to use the brush roller for carpets and a smoother roller (or none at all) for hard floors.

**Upright vacuums:** Switch to the carpet setting to engage the roller brush so it can lift debris off and out of the carpet fibers. Turn to the hard floor setting to disengage the brush when you're cleaning smooth floors to avoid scratching them.

**Cordless or canister vacuums:** If your vacuum has different flooring attachments, use the bristled brush for carpets and the one with a felt roller or silicone fins for hard floors.

## FOLLOW THE PATTERN

Years ago, a vacuum salesman showed me a technique that made our carpets look much cleaner. I've used it ever since. He explained that most of us vacuum our floors too quickly, leaving behind a lot of dirt. Any vacuum works better when used slowly, so the roller bar has time to pick up debris.

With carpeting, working slowly gives the roller time to part the fibers and reach the dirt between them. This leaves the telltale "vacuum lines" that housewives of the past used to be so proud of.

On hard floors, working slowly lets the roller lift the debris into the suction path instead of flinging it out the back. (If you've ever vacuumed up cat litter too quickly, you know exactly what I mean.)

So, the pattern for vacuuming goes slowly back and forth in overlapping strokes from one side of the room to the other. Then, if you're cleaning a carpet or area rug, turn at a right angle and do it again. This second pass hits the fibers from a different angle to get rid of even more dirt.

Give it a try. I bet you'll be as surprised by the improvement as I was all those years ago.

*Chapter Twelve*

# MOPPING MATTERS

*I* loathe mopping, so if I'm going to do it, I want to do it right. That means using the right mop at the right time with the right technique. (Then maybe taking a nap so the floor has plenty of time to dry.)

## MOPS FOR EACH FLOOR TYPE

In the past, there were only two options for mopping: doing it Cinderella-style on your hands and knees or using a string mop. Today, there are a variety of choices, and the right one depends on the type of flooring you have.

## FLAT

Flat mops with disposable pads like Swiffers are safe for all floor types and perfect for quick cleanups, but I'm not a fan of using them exclusively. Since they're expensive, most of us use them for too long and don't get the floor completely clean. You can test this after mopping by wiping a high-traffic spot like the area in front of your sink with a wet paper towel. Gross, right?

When you do use a disposable pad, flip it as soon as it starts turning gray from grime, and replace the pad entirely when the second side is dirty. That can mean going through several pads in one room, especially if you have pets. Plus, you always need a fresh one in the kitchen and a different one in the bathroom to avoid cross-contamination.

## STRING OR SPONGE

String mops and sponge mops are effective on tile, concrete, and linoleum. They get floors cleanest if you're good about rinsing and using a 2-bucket system. But they aren't good choices for wood, cork, or laminate because they use a lot of water, which can cause these types of floors to swell and warp.

Also, heads up if you have Oriented Strand Board (OSB) subfloors beneath tile or a floating floor like click-lock or LVP: excess water can seep through cracks or gaps between planks, and under baseboards along the wall. That will cause edge lifting and expensive, permanent damage. So, wring out that mop well and don't slosh water all over the floor no matter how cool it looks on Instagram.

## STEAM

Steam mops disinfect using hot, steamy water. They're not meant to be used with other cleaning products, because steam aerosolizes the ingredients. You don't want to inhale hot steamy vinegar, trust me.

Steam mops are ideal for tile and linoleum but check with the manufacturer if you have vinyl or LVP flooring. And don't use them wood or laminate floors because the combination of heat and moisture will damage them over time.

## SPRAY

Spray mops are user-friendly and let you control the amount of cleaning solution, so they're great for targeted cleaning. They give you flexibility in choosing the product to use, but make sure it's compatible with your flooring type.

Some spray mops use disposable pads, others use washables. Either way, remember to change the pad after each room or sooner if it gets visibly dirty.

## TO RINSE OR NOT TO RINSE?

Rinsing is basically mopping a second time with plain water. The frustrating thing is that product labels are often silent about whether you need to rinse them. If you measure exactly as the label directs and your floors look still dull or streaky, then add rinsing to your routine.

*Chapter Thirteen*

# WHAT'S IN MY CLEANING CLOSET?

I don't believe cleaning your home should cost a lot. I also don't think things have to be pretty or color-coordinated, they just need to work well.

So, I opt for affordable, natural, and multi-tasking over the latest trends. (That's probably why I'm a lousy "social media influencer." Bummer.) What follows is what I use to clean my home.

## CLEANING GLOVES

Gloves are non-negotiable when cleaning bathrooms since there are so many potentially dangerous germs. Sizing up makes them easier to get on and off. After cleaning, I leave them on and wash my hands with hot, soapy water then pop them outside to dry in the sun which disinfects them, too.

## OLD TOOTHBRUSHES

Toothbrushes are handy for cleaning nooks and crannies. Our dentist gives us new ones after every cleaning, so the old ones take a trip through the dishwasher before landing in my cleaning caddy. Clean them after use with soapy water. Then soak them in hydrogen peroxide for 15 minutes for disinfection, tap off the excess, and let them air dry.

## CLEANING CLOTHS

Microfiber cloths are my go-to for cleaning most surfaces. These cloths are made with twisted, split fibers which create more surface area than standard cloths. That design means they can trap more dust and do a better job scrubbing grime.

For other surfaces, I repurpose old white t-shirts and towels as either smooth polishing cloths (t-shirts) or absorbent stain removal rags (towels). Glass polishing cloths get one use before washing, but furniture polishing cloths get used a few times.

## ELECTROSTATIC DUSTERS

An electrostatic dusting head on an extension pole is great for high and hard-to-reach areas, like ceilings and the tops of bookcases. The older I get, the more I appreciate not having to climb step-stools or ladders to clean things!

Electrostatic dust mops make it easy to quickly clean hard floors—it takes just 5 minutes to pick up dust throughout my entire home. I use one from Bona that attaches to the flat mop head with Velcro strips.

Both tools are easy to clean. Shake them outdoors after use and wash in cold water then air dry as needed. To recharge the static any time, rub them quickly for several seconds with a plastic bag or nylon. That friction restores the static charge to attract and hold onto dust.

## FLOOR CLEANING TOOLS

A hand broom and dustpan are fine for quick pickups of dry messes or the initial cleanup after dropping a glass spray bottle, but I am otherwise not a fan of brooms indoors. Even careful sweeping sends dust and dirt into the air, plus there's always that annoying line when using a dustpan. Most of the time, I prefer a vacuum, but glass fragments are a definite exception.

Vacuum cleaners are a secret addiction of mine. I have a variety, from a cordless model for quick cleanups to an upright for deeper cleaning, a battery-powered shop vac for the car, and a robotic vacuum that cleans the kitchen after I go to bed. I even have a tiny vacuum to clean all the others, an idea I swiped without regret from Monica on *Friends*.

## MOPS

Three different mops round out my floor-cleaning gear. I keep a flat mop on hand for quick touch-ups as needed. For weekly cleaning everywhere but the kitchen, I use a spray mop and swap the pad out after each room.

I also use a string mop and two buckets in the kitchen every week, because I feel like it does the best job. About once a month, I use this in the other rooms, too.

## SPRAY BOTTLES

Spray bottles are must-haves if you make homemade cleaning solutions. I recently switched to glass bottles with a silicone wrap that serves two important purposes. First, it protects the contents from light which helps keep the ingredients effective. And it helps cushion the bottles if they get dropped or banged. (Guess how I learned that?)

## VINEGAR

Vinegar is a key ingredient in many of my homemade cleaners. White vinegar contains acetic acid, which is great for breaking down grease, killing mold and some bacteria, as well as eliminating odors. It's affordable, natural, and non-toxic.

Unless you're hypersensitive to smells, the odor fades as the acetic acid dries. My recipes use the standard 5% white vinegar available at grocery stores. I avoid apple cider vinegar because it contains pectin and proteins which can leave streaks.

## HYDROGEN PEROXIDE

Hydrogen peroxide (3%) lifts stains and brightens surfaces, and it's excellent for disinfecting and eliminating mold. It works by releasing oxygen bubbles on contact. These bubbles react with the proteins and DNA inside mold cells, causing oxidative damage to the cell membrane. The bubbles also help break up the mold structure, killing the mold and its spores.

These properties also make it useful on surfaces where vinegar isn't suitable, like natural stone or unfinished metals. For cleaning, the standard 3% hydrogen peroxide from the first aid section works well; anything stronger may cause damage. Keep it in the brown bottle it comes in, since exposure to light breaks down hydrogen peroxide over time.

*There's nothing magical about disinfecting wipes. I use hydrogen peroxide on a clean white cloth so I'm not throwing money away with the used wipe.*

## OLIVE OIL

Olive oil may seem like a strange cleaning ingredient until you think back to high school chemistry class where you learned "like dissolves like." Oil is great at dissolving stubborn oil-based things including dried paint, sticker residue, tree sap, crayon marks, and candle wax.

It's also good at getting through oil-based things like varnish or polish, so a good layer of it left overnight can remove white water rings on wood furniture. Warm it up first for best results and clean the area with a barely damp, soapy cloth afterward to remove any oily residue. (Mayo works, too, but I don't recommend keeping it in your cleaning closet. Trust me on this.)

## BAKING SODA

Baking soda (sodium bicarbonate) is made from the naturally occurring mineral trona. This powder makes an excellent gentle abrasive and can help absorb small spills. It has a high pH, which means it can neutralize acidic odor-causing molecules.

And, of course, the famous reaction between baking soda and vinegar produces a powerful fizzing reaction that cuts through grease and loosens stubborn grime.

## DISHWASHING LIQUID

Dishwashing liquid is my most frequently used cleaning supply. I think the internet has made us overthink what we need to use when cleaning, but soapy water is still the best for most washable household surfaces.

I use Dawn Original liquid (the spray gives me rashes), but if you prefer plant-based soaps just know they might leave streaks on shiny or glossy surfaces due to their oil content.

## ISOPROPYL ALCOHOL

Rubbing alcohol (isopropyl 70%), also known as "surgical spirits" in the U.K., acts as a solvent and disinfectant. As a solvent, isopropyl alcohol can dissolve oils, sugars, salts, and some adhesives. It evaporates quickly, so it can clean surfaces without leaving streaks and disinfect them, too. And it's inexpensive.

## ESSENTIAL OILS

Essential oils are optional. I don't get woo-woo about them, but some offer mild antibacterial properties and leave a pleasant scent. Since I have pets, I stick with lavender, chamomile, or cedar wood oil for their safety.

*Find all my homemade cleaning recipes on HousewifeHowTos.com*

## *Part Four*
# THE ASSIGNMENTS

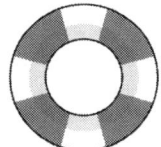

Before we get into the actual method, let's be clear: **this is not about constant cleaning**. Every time I suggest that some tasks should be done at least once daily while others are weekly, it leads to angry emails from people thinking I'm telling them to clean nonstop.

Nothing could be further from the truth.

Personally, I don't like cleaning. Tidying is more my game and there's a big difference between *consistent* tidying and *constant* cleaning.

- **Tidying** involves picking up after yourself and dealing with small messes before they become bigger ones.
- **Cleaning** involves tackling the bigger messes.

Yes, tidying up after yourself means not just bouncing out of a room and going to the next fun thing. But do you know who thinks it's okay to leave messes everywhere? Children. And it drives their parents mad.

You're not a child anymore. If you have kids, model the behavior you want and pick up after yourself. If you live with a partner, do the same. And if you live alone, guess what? You still need to pick up after yourself! That's not constant cleaning, it's being consistently considerate by not leaving a mess behind, and doing something about it when you do.

*If you consistently tidy, you won't need to constantly clean.*

Listen, I am a world-class complainer when I want to be, but I can tell you, complaining about having to clean a little each day won't get things any cleaner. Know what did it for me? Learning to pick up after myself combined with cleaning on a consistent schedule rather than a whim. Thanks to my ADHD, it was a struggle for me to learn all those years ago, but it made *all* the difference. In fact, it made me an expert.

So, if you're willing to learn a method that can help you keep your head above water, too, turn the page.

*Chapter Fourteen*

# KITCHEN CLEANING 101

Does it seem like every cleaning book says that the first step to having a clean kitchen is doing the dishes? Here's why.

When the sink is full, it's a hassle to rinse out a dishcloth so you can wipe up spills. Plus, new dishes can't fit in the sink and wind up on the counter. If there's food on them, it starts rotting or dries on, then it starts stinking and attracting pests.

Now, everyone else in your home sees a smelly, messy kitchen and figures leaving their trash or papers sitting around won't make a difference. Before you know it, the rest of your home starts stinking and looking bad, too.

So, if you want a cleaner kitchen, you have two options:

1. Do the dishes right away, or
2. Switch to paper plates, bowls, and cups.

Before you clutch those pearls in horror at my suggestion of using a disposable option, think back to the last time you were struggling to keep up with all the things you "should" do.

Maybe you were sick or injured, maybe you were fighting depression or anxiety, maybe you'd just had a baby, or you'd been having a rough time at work. Maybe all of them were going on at the same time.

Wouldn't it have made more sense if you'd just cut yourself some slack instead of "shoulding" all over yourself? There is no shame in taking an easy approach when you need it. Think of it like treading water: you're keeping afloat and alive.

If the potential environmental impact of using a biodegradable material like a paper plate bothers you, turn off the TV and lights an hour earlier and go to bed to make up for it. Either way, you'll feel better.

## THE QUICK WAY TO HAND-WASH DISHES

In 14 years of helping people learn to clean their homes better, I've had a lot complaints about the emphasis on starting with the dishes.

One woman came at me publicly in a video to say it's impossible to keep up with the dishes when you don't have a dishwasher. She even made a video which showed her filling half the divided sink with water, adding soap, then filling the other sink half for rinsing all *before* she began washing up. Well, I'd find that a hassle, too: it's not at all efficient!

If you've got to hand-wash dishes, keep a dish wand filled with liquid dish soap readily available, not hidden under the sink. Then, rinsing and scrubbing a glass or coffee cup takes less than two seconds—there's no reason for it to even sit in the sink.

Plates or silverware take maybe three seconds per piece. So washing a full place setting takes less than a minute. Got a family of five? It takes under 5 minutes to wash everything after a meal.

In other words, let's be honest that it's not always about the time it takes. Sometimes after planning, shopping for, and cooking a meal—then trying to enjoy it with kids squabbling or your significant other not acknowledging your effort—washing dishes afterward can feel overwhelming. I get it!

But remember what I said about paper plates. Seriously, they can be sanity-savers. If someone in your home has an issue with using them, let them do the dishes and give you a break. Or stop feeding them if they're old enough to cook. Either way, they'll get the point.

## KITCHEN HABIT CHAINS

Habit chains are a way to train yourself to do one action automatically after another. In the kitchen, here are the habit chains I rely on to keep messes under control.

1. Putting away groceries? Clear out expired foods.
2. Making a snack? Wipe the counter before eating it.
3. Cooking a meal? Put away ingredients after using them.
4. Putting something in the oven or on the stove? Wash the dishes you've used so far.
5. Finished eating? Wash the dishes.
6. Done with the dishes? Give the sink a quick rinse.
7. Wiping or washing anything? Wash out the sponge or dishcloth and let it air dry so it's ready for use.
8. Drying your hands? Change the towel if it feels damp.

If habit chains aren't your thing, then practice the 2-Minute Method once or twice a day. Set a reminder in your phone calendar or slap a sticky note where you'll see it. When you're ready to start, set a timer for two minutes and tidy up every mess you see. You may surprise yourself with how much you can get done in that time if you put some hustle in it.

## DAILY TIDYING

Habit chains prevent new messes and daily tidying resets a room to keep it consistently clean.

   **1. Empty the dishwasher or dish rack.** Starting your day with an empty dishwasher or sink makes it easier to stay on top of dishes. If they're full, dirty dishes will pile up in the sink and overflow onto the counter, making cleaning difficult.

   **2. Clean oven spills.** Sprinkle salt to absorb fresh spills and prevent cooking odors. Once the oven cools, wipe away the salt and you'll avoid a stubborn, baked-on mess.

   **3. Disinfect high-touch surfaces.** Reduce the risk of cross-contamination by wiping faucet handles, appliance controls, doorknobs, light switches, and remote controls. Use disinfecting wipes or hydrogen peroxide on a white cloth or paper towel.

   **4. Wipe down the counters and table.** Use a soapy rag, then disinfect where you prepare food. Disinfecting products need at least 5 minutes to work before you rinse or dry.

   **5. Run the garbage disposal.** With hot water running, turn on the disposal and add a small squirt of dish soap to clean and degrease the blades. Doing this every time you wash dishes, or at least at the end of the day, helps avoid clogs and odors.

   Need more oomph to deal with garbage disposal odors? Add some crushed ice cubes and salt before you turn it on, and they'll scour the blades for you.

   **6. Clean the sink daily.** Dirty sinks attract pests and are another source of cross-contamination. Wash yours at least once a day with hot, soapy water, using baking soda as an abrasive if needed. Then disinfect with hydrogen peroxide on porcelain sinks or rubbing alcohol on stainless steel.

**7. Clean high-traffic areas on the floor.** Run an electrostatic dust mop over the floor to pick up crumbs. Wipe up spills.

**8. Change the towels.** It's important to have two different towels for your kitchen: one for dishes and one for hands. Replace both at day's end or if they become grimy or damp.

**9. Empty the trash.** Take out the trash nightly to avoid pests. Before inserting a new bag, wipe spills in the can with a cleaning wipe.

## WEEKLY CLEANING

Some people prefer to clean their entire home in one day each week, while some like to tackle tasks randomly and check them off as they go. I'm a fan of room-based cleaning, so I focus on one room each weekday.

No matter your approach, here's what you need to clean in your kitchen at least once a week to keep the grease, grime, and food-borne germs under control.

**1. Clean the countertop and backsplash.** During the week we save time by cleaning around things. But now it's time to clean the things themselves to get rid of cooking grease and random splatters that collect dust. Then wipe the countertop and backsplash before putting everything back.

**2. Clean refrigerator shelves and drawers.** Move items aside and wipe the surfaces with a soapy rag then a disinfecting wipe or hydrogen peroxide on a white cloth. Line the drawers with paper towels to catch drips and control humidity, which helps your produce last longer.

**3. Wipe down appliances.** Pay extra attention to food stains on the stovetop since they can be fire hazards. Scour those with baking soda. For stubborn messes, lay a paper towel dampened with warm vinegar over the baking soda and wipe clean after the fizzing stops. Then add shine and fingerprint protection to stainless steel surfaces by buffing them with a little mineral oil on a soft cloth.

**4. Clean cabinet fronts.** A weekly wipe-down eliminates grease that attracts dust and looks grimy.

**5. Dust and polish.** Dust furniture, ceiling fans, and shelves weekly. I avoid spray polish in the kitchen, because the silicone in it can trap cooking grease and dust, leaving a sticky mess.

**6. Thoroughly clean the floor.** Vacuum along the base of walls with a crevice attachment, then switch to the floor attachment for the rest. Then mop the floor, starting at the far side of the room and cleaning your way out.

**7. Clean the trash can.** Use a soapy rag on spills and grime inside and out, then disinfect and let it air dry. Line the bottom of your trash can with junk mail or newspapers and a light sprinkling of baking soda before you add the new liner. They'll absorb spills and control odors, making it easier to clean.

## MONTHLY TASKS

Remember the buoy of housework? You've built a solid base in the kitchen with your daily tidying routine and developed a weekly cleaning routine that covers most areas. At the top are the occasional tasks that help it stay functional and organized.

To keep it easy, there are four weeks in a month, so four tasks to tack onto the weekly routine or knock out in one extra-long session.

**1. Wipe out cabinets and drawers.** If you have a large kitchen, tackle a few cabinets each week. On the cozy size? Do them all in one go. Either way, use the opportunity to declutter items you no longer use or like.

As your free up space, you may find it makes sense to rearrange things so they're near where you use them:

- Cooking utensils and pans close to the stove so you can grab them as needed.
- Food storage near countertops where you prepare meals.
- Tableware near the dishwasher or sink so it's easier to put away.
- Use the less convenient places, like the small cabinet above the fridge, for things you don't need to grab as often. (In my case, that's where I also keep the candy and the same logic applies.)

**2. Clean the oven.** Wiping down the inside of the oven is a breeze now that you're cleaning spills as they happen. All you need is a warm, soapy rag to remove grease, and another damp one to rinse away the soap residue.

Missed a spill? Scoop up whatever dried bits you can and apply a thick wet paste of baking soda and hot water to the spot. Let it dry and, as it does, it'll start loosening the food. Then lay a paper towel dampened with warm vinegar on top. Wait for that mini volcano to stop fizzing and wipe away the mess.

**3. Clean the dishwasher.** Some people swear by placing an upright coffee cup full of vinegar in the top rack when they're running the dishwasher. I do a few things first to get the dishwasher truly clean.

- Pull out the racks and wipe the interior, including the door gasket.
- Check the spinner arms and use tweezers to pull out anything stuck in the holes.
- Twist the filter to remove it, then give it a quick wash in the sink.

Now running it with that cup of vinegar can help degrease the drain line for an extra dose of clean.

**4. Dust from top to bottom.** Use an electrostatic duster to reach every spot—ceilings, walls, corners, and the space above your cabinets. Schedule this just before vacuuming and mopping, and you'll have a noticeably cleaner kitchen.

## 7 QUICK TIPS FOR A CLEANER KITCHEN

As the saying goes, "prevention is worth a pound of cure." So, if you don't enjoy making time to clean your kitchen, here are some ways to keep the messes down a bit.

**1. Keep steamy grease from escaping.** Any type of cooking with fats or oils releases grease into the air, which eventually settles on your kitchen surfaces, just like dust. To keep the mess contained, use a lid or splatter screen to keep the grease in the pan where it belongs.

**2. Filter the air while you cook.** Run your range hood or microwave vent fan when you're cooking to pull greasy steam through the filters. The metal mesh will trap the grease, so it doesn't land on your kitchen surfaces.

**3. Keep pests out of your food.** Using food storage containers isn't just about making your pantry look nice — it's about keeping food fresher and pest-free. Choose clear, stackable containers to save space.

**4. Make quick wiping even easier.** There's no need to complicate kitchen wipe-ups: keep a spray bottle full of water with a few drops of liquid dish soap on hand for easy all-purpose cleaning

## CLEANING 101

spray. Dump and replace it every couple of days so it doesn't get yucky.

**5. Tame the paperwork.** Anyone else feel like more papers sneak into their homes every time the door opens? I keep a shredder in the kitchen so it's easy to immediately shred junk mail instead of letting it pile up.

**6. Assign glasses.** Every family has that one person who fills a clean glass with water, takes a sip, and then leaves it in the sink. This drove me nuts for years until I cleared out our cabinet and kept just one glass per person, with a different color for each of us. That stopped the one-sip wonders! Now we use our personal glasses all day, and I'm not running the dishwasher nearly as often.

**7. Buy less food.** Bowls of colorful fruit turn into aspirational wastes of money if your family doesn't eat it all. Plus, you'll end up dealing with fruit flies. Shop carefully and buy only what you need: you'll save both time and money.

# Kitchen 101

## ☀ DAILY

- Empty dishwasher.
- Clean the sink.
- Run the disposal
- Disinfect handles.
- Wipe oven spills.
- Wipe table & counters.
- Touch up floor.
- Change towels.
- Take out trash.

##  WEEKLY

- Clear and clean counter & backsplash.
- Wipe appliance & cabinet fronts.
- Clean inside fridge.
- Dust furniture.
- Disinfect trash can.
- Vacuum & mop the floor.

## MONTHLY

- Clean inside oven.
- Clean inside cabinets & drawers.
- Clean inside dishwasher.
- Dust top to bottom.

## Chapter Fifteen
# LIVING SPACES CLEANING 101

*E*veryone seems to have different names for the room where they hang out with their loved ones: family room, TV room, media room, gathering room, great room, lounge, parlor, or the Jarl's Hall if you're a fellow *Skyrim* fan. I have nearly pulled out my hair trying to find one universal name for it.

In some homes, this room doubles as a place to entertain company. In others, there's a separate room for both purposes. Regardless of what you call it, we all want the same things here: a cozy space to share time with our family, and a place where we're proud to host guests. But keeping it clean can be a challenge.

## MANY HANDS AND EMPTY HANDS

My mother-in-law used to have a sign at her lake cabin which read "Many hands make light work." She explained it was to encourage her kids and grandkids to pitch in and help, so no one had to do all the work to make our get-togethers enjoyable.

As my kids like to say, I'm *extra*. So, we combined that with the "no empty hands" rule which says you never leave a room without taking your stuff with you.

The result? When many hands pick up their own stuff and put it away, everything stays cleaner. (Picture me doing that sassy emoji as you read this.)

That's too much to put on a sign, so we turned it into a family game: if you saw someone leave a room with empty hands, and you could find something they should've taken with them, they had to do one of your chores that week.

It caught on fast.

Two days after introducing the game, my daughter caught me walking around empty-handed. My penalty: I had to clean her room. Knowing they could make Mom or Dad do their least favorite chores kept the kids motivated to play, so they also stayed motivated to pick up after themselves. (We may or may not have intentionally let them catch us empty-handed for that reason. I'll never tell.)

## DROWNING IN CLUTTER

Clutter is like a rip tide: you think everything's fine, then you're pulled in deeper despite your best efforts to fight it. If you don't do something, it will overwhelm your space, leaving you feeling helpless and lost.

My ADHD means I must stay vigilant, or clutter will take over my home before I even notice. So, I've developed a surefire, no-fail strategy to keep it in check. Judging by the comments and unfollows I get when I share my method on social media, this solution is tough for many people. Here it is anyway: get rid of things. Yep, that's it.

Get. Rid. Of. Things.

Before you decide to start by getting rid of this book, hear me out. We all have reasons not to get rid of stuff. Most of them

## CLEANING 101

sound perfectly reasonable until we try explaining them to someone else.

> I'd feel bad if I got rid of it. It was a gift.

> From your spouse? Your kids? Your best friend?

> Um, no. It was from my ex-mother-in-law. Awful woman, but she gave good gifts.

> ...

> I'm going to use it someday.

> When?

> IDK but she left the price tag on. It wasn't cheap.

> Would you buy it for yourself?

> No, but I might need it someday.

> You've had it for years. Have you needed it? Ever?

> Well, no. Ok, I'll sell it so it's not a complete waste.

> You've years to do that. Why haven't you?

> Because if I get rid of it, I might wish I hadn't.

> You could say the same thing about the paper wrapper from yesterday's sandwich.

> But..

> Srsly?

## THE DOOM BOX DECLUTTERING METHOD

Have you heard of Doom Boxes before? They're a popular ADHD coping strategy. The acronym stands for "Didn't Organize, Only Moved" since they're usually filled with random things chucked inside to declutter a space. The idea is to quickly tidy up a space then go back to dealing with the contents of the box later.

That's often easier said than done.

I've filled multiple doom boxes with gifts I didn't like to avoid offending the giver. I've held onto items that remind me of loved ones just to avoid bringing bad luck. I've kept clothes that don't fit in case I gain or lose weight, and stuff for long-abandoned hobbies in case the interest returns. I've even kept a set of outdated encyclopedias so future generations of survivors can learn after a zombie apocalypse wipes out the power grid. I'm not kidding.

Look closely and you'll see that the same thing is behind every reason you and I hold onto clutter: *fear*. We're afraid of being wrong, of hurting others, of inconvenience, of lack, and of feeling foolish. (Also zombies.)

But at what cost? Too much clutter is oppressive. It stresses us out and makes it impossible to relax in our own homes. We start buying containers and shelving to make sense of all these things we're holding onto. Sometimes we go so far as to move to new homes with bigger storage areas, bigger house payments, and bigger tax bills.

No matter the size of our home, cleaning takes longer because there's so much stuff in our way. Then, the psychological friction caused by having to move things before we can clean makes us put it off. Before long, the mess feels overwhelming.

And what do stressed, overwhelmed people do? They buy more stuff to make themselves feel better!

*See the cycle?*

I didn't start feeling in control of clutter until I gave myself permission to start giving things away. And by *giving*, I mean literally putting it in a pile at the end of my driveway and announcing on local social media that it was there.

Oh, I thought about a garage sale but kept putting it off. I tried Facebook Marketplace a few times, but people kept no-showing. But when I posted one announcement about it being free? That pile of stuff was gone within the hour. I wasn't making money trying to sell it, so why not just get it out of my house?

Does it seem silly or wasteful to give away things when I could make money from them? To me it seems *more* silly to hold onto things when they're making me miserable in my own home. It feels *more* wasteful letting clutter weigh me down with so much shame that I can't have people over and can't even relax.

By fighting my fear of regret, I saved myself from drowning in clutter. It was hard and exhausting at first. But like swimming laps (what did you think I was done talking about swimming?), the more often I did it, the better I got at it.

But if giving away your clutter seems like too big of a step, here's an alternative that turns it into a memorable lesson. I call it my DOOM BOX DECLUTTERING METHOD:

1. Pick a room and pack up anything you haven't used in the past year. Add other things you've been thinking about getting rid of, which you're tired of seeing, or which just get on your nerves. (Things, not people, please.)
2. Tape the box shut and write the date on the outside.
3. Repeat in every room.

4. Now, load up your car and drive the boxes to a storage facility. Rent the space for a year.
5. If you haven't needed anything from the boxes by the end of the year, haul them to the thrift store. Do not stop to open the boxes and stroll down memory lane: drop them off unopened.

Seems silly to go to all that trouble and expense, doesn't it? But you're going through trouble and expense already! Having to dig through clutter to find things or move stuff so you can clean is a time-wasting hassle. Having to buy more bins and organizers or books to get your clutter under control is an actual expense.

So, if the fear of being wrong about getting rid of something is what's holding you back, give the Doom Box Decluttering Method a try. You'll likely find you have nothing to be afraid of and just one question to answer at the end of paying to store all that stuff for a year: *was it worth it?*

## LIVING SPACE HABIT CHAINS

Like any married couple, my husband and I had our share of disagreements, but twenty years later one stands out: the day I complained he'd left his stuff in the family room, which made it take longer to clean.

"Your stuff is sitting out, too," he said.

I pointed out that I knew I had to put my things away before cleaning it was *his* stuff that was in my way.

"So tell me when you're going to clean. I'll put my things away when you do."

When I'd finally cooled down, I saw my purse on a chair, bottles of nail polish on the coffee table, and magazines on the floor next to the sofa. To me, putting these away was the first step in my cleaning process. To my family, my stuff was sitting out, so why wasn't their stuff okay, too?

Later, I share more about how I got everyone in the family on board with keeping the house tidy. The short version is that I started following habit chains in the living room. If you're constantly seething over how messy your shared living spaces get, try putting these to work in your home.

1. Done watching TV? Straighten the throw pillows and blankets on the sofa.
2. Kids finished playing? Have them put away toys before they go onto the next thing.
3. Spilled something? Pause your show and clean it ASAP.
4. Just passing through? No empty hands!
5. Heading to bed? Take your stuff with you.

## DAILY TIDYING

Have you ever started a day with plenty of time and energy for cleaning, only to find yourself suddenly out of one or both? With my psoriatic arthritis, I've experienced days where everything's fine for an hour or two, then *WHAMMO!* I can barely make it to the sofa.

This has taught me to prioritize my daily tidying by starting with the kitchen to avoid contamination or pests. Next, I focus on the living room to create a comfortable, calming spot to rest. I like to think of it as a proactive form of emergency self-care.

So, the daily tidying acts like a quick reset, making sure the room looks just-cleaned even when it's not.

1. Straighten sofa cushions, fluff throw pillows and fold blankets.
2. Spot clean any small messes or spills.
3. Go over high-touch surfaces like door handles, light switches, and the TV remote with a disinfecting wipe.
4. Tidy up magazines, games, toys.
5. Put away things that belong in other rooms, including dishes and trash.
6. Wipe off tables and straighten the stuff on them.
7. Clean the high-traffic areas on the floor as needed.

I use a cleaning caddy to make daily tidying easier. It's stocked with microfiber cloths, a spray bottle of soapy water, disinfecting wipes and an empty trash bag. Then I can grab the caddy and buzz through all the rooms in one go.

## WEEKLY CLEANING

If you have an entirely different room for entertaining guests, you may not need to spend much time cleaning it every week if you don't have people over much. But don't skip it altogether: dust collects in unused rooms and gets harder to remove over time.

**1. Dust from top to bottom.** Here's the beauty of cleaning consistently each week: you don't have to overthink dusting. Instead of climbing ladders, you can put your extension duster to work cleaning ceiling fan blades and then use it in long vertical strokes on walls and doors, trim and baseboards. That means you're only doing the furniture and shelves by hand with a damp cloth, so it all goes much faster.

**2. Vacuum soft seating.** Take the cushions off and use the crevice attachment to vacuum the gaps around the seating platform. Switch to the upholstery attachment and vacuum the seating area, the backrest and the arms. Next, clean each cushion before you put it back.

**3. Spot clean carpet and upholstery stains.** Most food grime or dirt just needs a little cool, soapy water on a white cloth. For greasy stains, make it warm water instead. Avoid saturating the cushion or you'll wind up with hidden mold.

Before spot cleaning, check inside a cushion for fabric care labels. W means the fabric is washable with water. S means use a solvent (like rubbing alcohol), not water. W/S means you can use either. And an X means to take it to a professional.

**4. Polish glass surfaces.** Use a fresh, dry cloth and switch as soon as it feels damp, so you don't leave streaks. For glass tabletops and windows your pets press their noses against, use a soapy rag first then buff the area dry before polishing.

**5. Wash throw blankets and pet beds.** Even if no one in your family uses the sofa blankets like a napkin when they're snacking in front of the TV, they still collect dust and other debris—especially if you have pets. Regular washing keeps dust down and odors away.

**6. Vacuum the floor.** Start with the crevice attachment around the edges of the room and base of heavy furniture like bookshelves. Then work in the pattern I described earlier.

**7. Mop hard floors.** Make a point to vacuum and mop on the same day to keep dust from settling and creating streaks.

## MONTHLY TASKS

Four weeks, four monthly tasks. Nifty!

**1. Vacuum the furniture details.** Tilt the sofa and chairs forward if you can and vacuum the floor underneath them. While you've got them tipped, vacuum the underside of your furniture: spiders love building webs there.

**2. Vacuum the other tricky spots.** Use the dust attachment and clean along the tops of books and where their spine rest on the shelf, two places where dust collects. Then use it on your lampshades, woven décor and wicker.

**3. Wash throw pillow covers.** Unzip throw pillow covers and follow the laundering instructions on the label. Refresh the inserts by either fluffing them in the dryer or letting them air outside for an hour or two.

**4. Declutter and organize storage.** Take some time to go through drawers, cabinets, or entertainment units. Organize the contents and discard or donate items that are no longer needed or used.

## MAXIMALISM AND WISHING FOR MIRACLES

When I was growing up, people either tried to make their homes look like something out of *Dynasty* or *Dallas*, or they covered every possible surface with a French Country duck. (Seriously, they were everywhere.)

Gen Z is bringing back many Gen X styles like neon, corset belts, and shoulder pads, but fortunately they aren't reviving the over-the-top décor. (Or the ducks.) Minimalism is in, and considering how much busier life is now than it was in the '80s, the pared-back look is likely to stay.

Listen, I adore the maximalist style too, but it makes cleaning so much harder! Knickknacks gather dust. The more stuff on display, the longer it takes to clean. No amount of wishing can change that. Guess who's tried?

Plus, all that excess also means family members may not see the difference between decorative items and everyday clutter. That apothecary jar collection on the coffee table full of dried flowers and wooden beads? Looks stunning to me. To my family, it's just stuff. And if I can leave stuff sitting out, they figure they should be able to as well. The nerve.

So, this might not be what you want to hear, but the more collections, framed photos, dried floral arrangements, figurines, baskets, souvenirs, and other decorations you have on display, the dustier your home will be and the longer it will take to clean.

If you enjoy having things on display, treat it as a curated collection. Either stash them in glass-front cabinets to keep the dust off, or rotate what you've got sitting out every month or two like a museum does with its exhibits.

Otherwise, you'll have to learn to love dust. I know which I'd prefer.

# Living Room 101

## ❖ DAILY

- Straighten cushions.
- Fold blankets.
- Spot clean spills.
- Put away clutter.
- Disinfect high-touch areas.
- Tidy & wipe off tables.
- Touch-up floor.

##  WEEKLY

- Dust.
- Wash blankets.
- Vacuum sofas & chairs.
- Treat stains.
- Polish glass.
- Clean the floor.

## MONTHLY

- Vacuum details.
- Declutter drawers, cabinets.
- Wash pillow covers.
- Vacuum under furniture.

© 2024 Kate Berry

## Chapter Sixteen
# BEDROOM CLEANING 101

Stress shows up differently in everyone's life. For me, it first appears in my bedroom. When I'm stressed, I'm either too busy or too tired to tidy up, so I start dumping things onto the dresser or floor.

Making my bed would probably get skipped, too, but I have an elderly cat who sees an unmade bed as an invitation to hawk up hairballs.

Once I started prioritizing habit chains and daily bedroom tidying, it went from reflecting my stress levels to being a room I looked forward to seeing at the end of the day. That didn't come easily, though.

### HABIT CHAINS IN BEDROOMS

If you wake up clear-headed, or have the luxury of going at your own pace in the morning, good habit chains can tidy up your bedroom before you leave it.

1. Waking up? Throw the covers back so the mattress airs out.
2. Finished showering? Make the bed while your moisturizer sinks in.
3. Getting dressed? Put your pajamas in the hamper or on a hook.
4. Finished dressing? Open the curtains and crack open the windows for a few minutes.
5. Leaving the room? Grab anything that belongs somewhere else.
6. Going to bed? Put away anything sitting out on the dresser or nightstand before you shut off the light.

## DAILY TIDYING

For those of us who don't wake up feeling brimming with Disney Princess energy, a daily tidying routine might be the way to go.

**1. Air out your bed.** Give it at least 30 minutes with the covers pulled back to release your body heat and dry out any sweat. You'll prevent dust mites and mattress odors.

**2. Open your curtains or blinds.** Dark bedrooms are havens for spiders and mold, so throw open those curtains and let in some sunlight every morning.

**3. Air out your room.** While you've got the curtains open, open the window for at least 5 minutes to help refresh the air and reduce indoor pollutants. If you have allergies, avoid opening windows for an hour before and after sunrise and sunset — plants release the most pollen during these times.

**4. Make your bed.** Once your mattress has had time to air out, make your bed so your sheets don't gather dust. (Or your cat's hairballs.) A made bed also makes your entire room look neater.

**5. Tidy up the flat surfaces.** Put away things that belong in drawers or closets, toss any trash, and return items to other rooms.

**6. Clean high-traffic areas.** High-traffic areas in the bedroom are basically the path around your bed and from it to the door. If you have hard floors, use a dust mop. If you have carpet, pick up the big chunks of debris daily and use a vacuum just on these spots every couple of days.

## WEEKLY CLEANING

With habit chains preventing messes and daily tidying resetting the room, there isn't much to the weekly bedroom cleaning. I'm usually done in 15-20 minutes.

**1. Dust thoroughly, from top to bottom.** Start with an electrostatic duster and work top to bottom in long, sweeping strokes to pick up dust: walls, door and window trims, sills and sashes, picture frames, shelves, hard furniture, and baseboards. Switch to a damp microfiber cloth to wipe the furniture.

**2. Disinfect high-touch areas.** Use disinfecting wipes on door handles, dresser and nightstand handles, light switches, and if you have one, the TV remote.

**3. Empty and clean the trash can.** Wipe it inside and out with a disinfecting wipe then replace the liner once it's dry.

**4. Clean glass surfaces.** Polish the insides of windows, mirrors, and any glass décor to keep things sparkling. Remember: damp rags leave streaks, so switch as needed.

**5. Change your sheets.** If you use a flat and fitted set, swap both for clean ones. Just a fitted sheet and covered duvet? You can probably wash the duvet cover every two weeks unless you've got pets or allergies.

**6. Vacuum all areas.** Start with the attachments around the base of the walls then switch to the floor attachment. Follow the pattern for carpets and don't forget the area under your bed!

**7. Mop hard floors immediately after vacuuming.** Start at the far side of the room and mop your way out the door for best results.

## MONTHLY TASKS

Again, there are four once-a-month bedroom tasks. I rotate them by doing one each week, but do what works for you.

**1. Vacuum the mattress.** Use the upholstery attachment and work top to bottom, then side to side to get as much dust and debris out of the surface as possible. Switch to the crevice attachment and go around the edges where there's piping, and where your mattress rests on the bed platform, box spring or slats.

**2. Wash decorative pillow covers and throws.** Unzip the cover and check the care label then follow the instructions. No label? Leave the inserts and covers outside, separately, to air out.

**3. Freshen the bed covering or duvet insert.** Hang your duvet insert, comforter or bedspread outside to air it out naturally. Or fluff it in the dryer for 5 minutes without heat to get rid of dust, pet hair, and odors.

**4. Tidy up inside drawers.** Dump out each drawer, get rid of any clutter, then wipe the drawer interior. Sort the contents before putting everything away neatly.

## REDUCING BEDROOM DUST

Does it feel like your bedroom gets dusty faster than any other room in your home? There's a reason: you!

All the dead skin cells and hair shed in your sleep and any dirt on your shoes turn to dust. Add in blanket and carpet fluff plus pet hair and it can feel like you're sleeping in a cloud of it. (If you aren't cleaning your bedroom thoroughly at least once a week, you probably are.)

Even if you don't have allergies, dust can disrupt your sleep and leave your nose and throat feeling scratchy. If you're sensitive, it can feel like little bugs landing on your skin — hard to sleep well with that going on! So here are some tips to put the Do Not Disturb mode on dust in your bedroom.

### Moisturize

A good layer of lotion, head to toe, helps keep your skin hydrated and reduces flaking, which reduces dust. Bonus if you bathe first since that gets rid of dirt, pollen, and dead skin cells, too.

### Brush before bed

Shed hair is dead hair, and dead things turn into dust. So, give your own hair a quick brush in the bathroom before bed. If you have pets, give them a once-over outside at least once a week.

### No bedroom dry-cleaning

Dust in your room settles on your bed just like it does on the floor. A quilt or bedspread that isn't washed regularly is more dusty than the floor, which gets cleaned weekly. That's why all bedding should be washable, ideally in hot water, to eliminate dust mites and allergens.

### Replace old fabrics

Textiles and fabrics wear out and break down. Old sheets and curtains, even old carpeting adds fluff and fibers to the air which turn into dust. In general, synthetic fabrics wear out in 2-3 years; cotton and bamboo last 3-5 years; and high-quality linen lasts 5-10 years when properly cared for.

### Clean the air

Maintaining good air quality in your bedroom can be a balancing act that pays off. In dry, winter months a humidifier does for bedroom furnishings what moisturizer does for your skin: it keeps things from drying out and disintegrating, which leads to dust.

Using an air purifier year-round keeps the dust down, too. You can even get a combo unit but, whatever you choose, follow the manufacturer's schedule for cleaning and HEPA filter replacement so you're not adding mold to your air.

### Skip under-bed storage

Using the space under your bed for storage is convenient, but it can also provide a breeding ground for dust mites. Keeping that area clear promotes air circulation, which keeps your mattress cooler while you sleep.

If you must store things beneath your bed, use hard-sided, lidded containers and wipe them down weekly. This will help keep dust and dust mites at bay.

**MINIMIZE.**

If you rolled your eyes when I mentioned this earlier, at least consider a minimalist approach in your bedroom. A dusty bedroom can lead to itchy, red eyes and stuffy noses, resulting in poor sleep. Ultimately, you'll need to decide which you'd rather have look good: you or your room.

# Bedroom 101

## DAILY
- Air out bed.
- Open curtains.
- Air out room.
- Tidy tables, dresser.
- Make bed.
- Touch up floor.

## WEEKLY
- Dust.
- Disinfect high-touch surfaces.
- Clean trash can.
- Polish glass & wood.
- Change sheets.
- Clean the floor.

## MONTHLY
- Tidy drawers.
- Freshen bedcover.
- Wash pillow covers.
- Vacuum the mattress.

© 2024 Katie Berry

*Chapter Seventeen*
# BATHROOM CLEANING 101

The bathroom is one place where cleanliness isn't a matter of opinion or personal taste. With the high potential for bacteria and mold, maintaining hygiene is essential for health and safety.

So, when I recommend cleaning and then disinfecting a surface, it's not about creating extra work — it's about protecting you and your family.

Cleaning removes visible dirt, but it also prepares the surface for disinfecting. Disinfectants need about 5 minutes to do their job, a period known as "dwell time." If you apply disinfectant to a surface that hasn't been cleaned, the effectiveness is reduced. Then no matter how long you leave it, it can't fully wipe out harmful bacteria like E. coli, staph, strep, and MRSA.

That's why it's a two-step process: clean first to reduce the germ load, and then disinfect to eliminate the remaining bacteria.

## BATHROOM HABIT CHAINS

Bathrooms are boring. I tend to plan out my day in the shower and often compose entire emails (and arguments) in my head while brushing my teeth. My brain is anywhere *but* in that room.

Sound familiar? That's one of the reasons our bathrooms get cluttered so quickly: we aren't even aware of the mess we're leaving behind.

When I first began using habit chains as part of my morning routine, I was amazed how little time it takes to put away messes instead of leaving them. Within days, my bathroom began looking better.

1. Finished brushing your teeth? Rinse the sink to get rid of toothpaste spots.
2. Ready to shower? Turn on the fan to keep the air circulating.
3. Done showering? Squeegee the shower walls to prevent water spots and soap scum.
4. Finished putting on makeup? Sweep your cosmetics into a basket and put it away to keep your counter clear.
5. Done getting ready? Grab a cleaning wipe and go over the faucets and counter.
6. Leaving the bathroom? Turn off the exhaust fan.

A two-minute session after you're done getting ready for the day can accomplish the same thing, though you might want to slap a sticky note on the mirror to remind yourself.

## DAILY TIDYING

No time to tidy as you go in the morning (no pun intended)? Here's the quick routine to reset your bathroom daily in less time than it takes for your sunscreen to dry.

1. **Wipe the counters.** Wiping counters with a dry cloth after a steamy shower makes clean-up go fast. Use it on the faucets and then the countertops to get rid of hair, dust, and makeup debris.

2. **Rinse the sinks.** Get rid of the toothpaste globs and soap splatters before they harden. You'll save loads of scrubbing time later on.

3. **Stop shower mold.** Use a squeegee to prevent mold and soap scum buildup. Leaving the shower door or curtain slightly open helps air circulate and speeds up drying, reducing mold risk.

4. **Hang up or change towels.** Hand towels easily spread germs, so change them at least once a day, or sooner if they feel damp. Bath towels develop mold and mildew spores that can cause skin rashes and infections, so change them every other use.

5. **Shake out the bathmat.** Hang up towel-type mats and shake out small rugs so they dry faster and stay cleaner.

6. **Touch up the floor.** Wipe around the toilet with a disinfecting wipe. (You know why.) Then go over it again with a fresh one for a double-clean guarantee.

## WEEKLY CLEANING

Tidying as you go and daily touch-ups make weekly cleaning much easier. I used to dread cleaning the bathrooms in my home (especially the kids' bathroom), but daily tidying has cut the time required for weekly cleaning in half.

1. **Get the air going.** Run the exhaust fan and open any windows to whisk away airborne nasties.

2. **Gather the washables.** Round up all towels and bathmats

and get a load of wash going.

**3. Clear and wipe countertop items.** Start clearing your bathroom counter and wipe off things as you set them aside.

**4. Wipe high-touch points.** Grab a fresh soapy rag and wipe the cabinet fronts, handles, and doorknobs.

**5. Spray and wipe.** Wash sinks, counters, tub, shower, and toilet. Use a soapy rag for this, since you'll be disinfecting next.

**6. Disinfect.** Now that these germy surfaces are clean, apply your disinfectant and wait 5 minutes for it to knock out germs. Rinse as needed. (I use the waiting time to start laundering the towels.)

**7. Clean and disinfect the toilet bowl.** Apply your toilet bowl cleaner and let it sit a few minutes before scrubbing and flushing to rinse. If your toilet is heavily stained, or if someone using it has been ill, repeat the process for added disinfection.

**8. Mirror and glass polish.** Sparkle up mirrors and glass fixtures with a fresh cloth and your favorite glass cleaner.

**9. Trash duties.** Empty the trash can, wipe it with a soapy rag, then disinfect it. Replace the liner when it's dry.

**10. Sweep and mop.** Vacuum or sweep the floor first, then mop with a disinfecting floor cleaner. Leave the fan going to circulate air and help your floor dry, too.

## MONTHLY TASKS

Four weeks, four monthly tasks. These are best done *before* you start the week's cleaning session.

**1. Dust from the top down.** Use an extension duster and clean in long, sweeping strokes. Start with the exhaust fan cover and work your way to baseboards.

**2. Tackle wall smudges.** Wipe the walls with a warm, soapy rag. You might want to go over the ones near the toilet with a disinfecting wipe, too — thank you, boys!

**3. Declutter cabinets.** Toss expired or unused items. Unlike you, that clutter is not getting better with age. Make like Elsa in *Frozen* and let it go.

**4. Clear the drains.** Tackle odors and buildup in your drains with a monthly de-clog: sprinkle ½ cup baking soda in the drain followed by 1 cup warm vinegar. Do this with all of the drains at the same time (tub, shower and sinks) and cover the openings to keep the fizzing in the pipes where it can bust through grime. Then turn the hot water on for all of them at the same time to send gunk down and out your mainline.

## KEEPING MOLD AND MILDEW AT BAY

Not all mold is dangerous to humans. For example, blue cheese gets its distinctive look (and smell) from mold, and it's quite delicious. A relative of this mold is also the basis for the common antibiotic penicillin which isn't edible but is still a good thing. But mold doesn't have to be dangerous to humans to be dangerous to your home.

Mold is a fungus that feeds on materials like wood, drywall, and grout. As it spreads, it breaks down these materials, weakening walls, floors, and ceilings. It also deteriorates caulk and grout around plumbing, leading to leaks that make the problem worse.

And mold *loves* bathrooms. All that moisture from showers and baths, even just flushing the toilet or leaving the lid open, means bathrooms are constantly at risk. To protect the health of your family and integrity of your home, it's important to stay on guard against the stuff.

## Prioritize Air Circulation

Moving air dries surfaces faster by speeding up evaporation. So, either keep your bathroom window open on dry days, or run your bathroom's exhaust fan for at least 15 minutes after every shower to get rid of the steamy air. No exhaust fan? Use a small wall-mounted fan plugged into a GFCI outlet for safety.

## Dry Your Shower

Use a squeegee or towel on the shower walls and doors after every use. If you use a shower curtain, shake off the excess water first. Then leave the shower door or curtain partially open so air can circulate. A doorstop or wedge can help with pivoting doors.

## Hang Towels and Bathmats

Bath linens can't dry out if they're in a heap. Besides mold and mildew, they'll attract pests like silverfish. Also, eww.

## Check for Leaks Routinely

Fix any issues with wobbly or dripping faucets promptly. Even slow, small leaks from a failing seal or hairline crack can cause significant damage.

I make it a habit to check the pipes when decluttering the bathroom cabinets each month. In the twenty years I've lived in my home, I've caught more than one failing seal under our sinks before it led to a big problem, so that's a practice I'm never going to give up.

Every few months, it's also a good idea to put a piece of tissue on the floor next to the toilet overnight to see if there's any leakage from the wax seal.

**CLEANING 101**

## Declutter

The more items sitting on bathroom surfaces, the more spots there are gathering moisture and the more opportunities for mold to grow. Put things away in cabinets and drawers when you're not using them, so they don't collect damp. It'll be easier to wipe off your countertops when there's less clutter, too.

# Bathroom 101

### 🍋 DAILY
- Wipe counters.
- Rinse sinks.
- Squeegee shower.
- Hang up towels.
- Shake out mat.
- Touch up floor.

### 🏖️ WEEKLY
- Clear and clean sinks, counters, tub/shower & toilet.
- Disinfect in same order.
- Scrub toilet bowl.
- Polish glass.
- Clean trash can.
- Clean the floor.

### 🐚 MONTHLY
- Dust top to bottom.
- Clean the drains.
- Clean wall smudges.
- Declutter cabinets & drawers.

© 2024 Katie Berry

## Chapter Eighteen
# ENTRYWAY 101

First impressions matter, and a messy entryway can create a bad one. But let's be real: people don't spend a lot of time in your entryway unless you've got a butler parking them there while he asks if you're receiving company.

So, don't stress about it. If your entryway is safe and tidy, you're doing well.

## DAILY TIDYING

The more people using your entryway, and the closer it is to ground level, the messier it'll get. Big family in a farmhouse? You already know you're fighting dirt and clutter here every day. Here's how to quickly tidy it up.

**1. Contain the shoes.** A boot tray catches dirt when people take off their shoes at the door.

**2. Clear out clutter.** Everyone tends to put things down as soon as they walk into their homes: purses, book bags, the shopping or mail. To keep clutter under control, buzz through the area daily to find what's out of place and put it away.

3. **Disinfect high-touch areas.** Even if you don't have a lot of visitors, a quick wipe with a disinfecting cloth on doorknobs, handles, light switches, and handrails provides some extra peace of mind.

4. **Tidy the entry mats.** A daily shake outdoors helps keep the dirt where it belongs. If you live in a very dusty area, consider hosing down or dumping a bucket of water on the front step to remove extra dirt, too.

5. **Touch up the floor.** The electrostatic dust mop is my best friend here: it takes 2 seconds to pick up a day's worth of dog hair and dirt. Then a damp rag touches up any spots.

## WEEKLY CLEANING

If you live solo in a city skyscraper, you can probably get by with just a weekly cleaning. Otherwise, work this into your routine to keep your entryway looking good for guests and feeling like a hearty welcome when you come home.

1. **Dust from top to bottom.** Get those tricky, high spots with the extendable electrostatic duster. Switch to a damp microfiber cloth for railings, furniture and decor.

2. **Freshen the front door.** Wash the door and threshold with a soapy rag, rinse, then dry it with a soft towel.

3. **Polish glass.** To avoid streaks, clean glass surfaces like storm doors when the sun isn't directly shining on them.

4. **Vacuum and mop.** Sweep off the front step, shake out the mats, then vacuum and mop the interior floor thoroughly.

## MONTHLY TASKS

A task for each week of the month. Surprise!

1. **Deep clean the front step.** Remove everything from the front step and sweep it thoroughly. Hose down the step and the

surrounding area. Scour stubborn spots on cement with a paste of baking soda or powdered oxygen bleach and water to clean stubborn grime. These are safe around pets and plants.

**2. Clean wall smudges.** Remove marks on doors, walls, and trim with warm, soapy water. Cleaning walls from the bottom up helps avoid drips that can leaves grimy streak marks on paint.

**3. Clean the light fixtures.** Give indoor and outdoor fixtures a cleaning to eliminate dust and dead bugs. Clean lights given an instant boost of curb appeal.

**4. Refresh outdoor decor.** Use a dry paintbrush to dust wreaths and wicker. For other items, a simple soapy wash will do.

## MY TAKE ON THE NO-SHOES RULE

Imagine a guest in your home dropped their pants and pooped in the living room. Are you a bad host for finding that unpleasant or gross? Are you controlling for telling them that's not acceptable?

Yet some people freak out when they're asked to remove their shoes when visiting someone's home. This seems to be primarily a U.S. thing: in many other cultures, you're raised to remove them as a sign of respect for the home's occupants.

That's because shoes worn outdoors walk though all sorts of messes like bacteria, pollen, road salt, grease, dirt, and poop.

If you're someone who doesn't automatically remove their shoes when visiting people, that's what you're smearing around on the floors of people who've invited you into their home. Why would you drag that inside?

Think about it: some people have compromised immune systems, some have severe allergies. Some have little kids who crawl around. Some can't afford to fix scratches left by rocks caught in the sole of your sneakers. They're not asking you to clean their homes, they're just asking you not to drag nasty stuff indoors and trash their place.

And if you're someone who doesn't want others wearing shoes inside, don't feel bad about asking. You're entitled to protect your health and property. But understand, many people don't like walking around barefoot (especially if you aren't cleaning the floors every day) or they worry their feet might smell.

So, keep a basket of washable slipper socks or disposable shoe covers near the door. "Would you prefer slipper socks or shoe covers?" is a great way to bring up the topic.

See? Manners work in both directions: guests don't have to go barefoot, but you don't have to take crap from inconsiderate people in your own home, either.

# Entryway 101

###  DAILY

- Contain the shoes.
- Clear out clutter.
- Disinfect high-touch surfaces.
- Shake mats outside.
- Touch up floor.

###  WEEKLY

- Dust top to bottom.
- Wipe down the door & threshold.
- Polish glass.
- Clean the floor.
- Sweep the step.

### MONTHLY

- Wash the front step & mats.
- Clean wall smudges.
- Clean light fixtures.
- Refresh outdoor decor.

*Chapter Nineteen*

# HOME OFFICE 101

I work in my home office every day and it also houses my book collection. So I confess, my home office is the one place I don't mind letting my inner messy gal have free rein.

Mostly that's because, as a writer, I've learned to leave my desk mid-sentence. If I'm on a roll, I don't tidy so the next day I can resume exactly where I left off without wondering what comes next. If I'm not in the middle of a project, I'll tidy things a little but leave the bulk of the cleaning for the end of the week.

## DAILY TIDYING

If you don't use your home office every day, you may only need the weekly cleaning.

**1. Pick up clutter.** From crumpled notes on the floor to dishes that belong in the kitchen, the less clutter in your office the easier it is to clean.

**2. Tidy up.** I like leave my office all set for the next morning: notepad and pen front and center, keyboard and mouse near the monitor, nothing else in the way. If you only use your desk to pay bills, reduce psychological friction by making sure what you need is there and ready to go.

**3. Disinfect the keyboard and mouse.** Do you need to wipe your keyboard and mouse daily with a disinfecting cloth? Probably not, unless you snack or eat lunch at your desk. I do, so I make it a daily habit.

## WEEKLY CLEANING

Going screen-free every weekend is my goal, even though I'm not always successful. Cleaning my office on Fridays makes it more likely, since I have to shut down the computers to do it.

**1. Sort the papers.** I shred junk mail as it comes in I'm a firm believer that if I can easily get a copy of a document, I don't need to keep one in my home. So filing takes just a few seconds.

**2. Clean the electronics.** Monitors generate static electricity which attracts dust. The best way to get rid of it is with a barely damp cloth then buff until it's dry. Never use glass cleaner on monitors, not even those with retina glass, since it has a coating that is easily corroded.

**3. Dust everything.** That electrostatic duster makes dusting the office a breeze. I work in long strokes top to bottom to get the ceiling, light fixtures, corners and trim, plus the tops and spines of books and the shelves. Then I switch to a damp microfiber cloth and wipe the rest.

**4. Polish the shiny stuff.** You know the drill: clean the inside of windows, glass knickknacks, and metal accents. If polishing furniture, use a fresh cloth. But remember, no more than once a month to avoid waxy buildup.

**5. Clean the floor.** Use the attachments at the bottom of walls, under furniture, and beneath any cushions. Then vacuum the rest of the floor and mop.

## MONTHLY TASKS

Seven monthly tasks this time. Just kidding, still only four.

**1. Empty the shredder.** On Fridays, I run a sheet of ultra-fine sandpaper (000 grit) through my shredders to keep the blades sharp. Using a plastic shopping bag as a liner makes emptying them weekly a breeze.

**2. Clean the window treatments.** Use the vacuum's dust brush vertically on curtains, horizontally on blinds. Then go over blinds with a damp cloth to get anything you missed.

**3. Vacuum books and details.** Thoroughly vacuum lampshades, throw pillows, and other tricky details. Once a month, I vacuum the front and tops of my books then pull them forward and vacuum behind them, too. With over a thousand volumes, this isn't a quick task but it helps protect my collection from silverfish.

**4. Wipe wall smudges and trim.** Run a soapy rag around the doorknobs, trim, near the light switches, and anywhere else you see smudges.

# Home Office 101

###  DAILY

- Throw away trash.
- Straighten items on desk.
- Put away clutter.
- Disinfect keyboard, mouse.

###  WEEKLY

- Sort, file and shred paperwork.
- Clean electronics.
- Dust top to bottom.
- Polish glass & wood.
- Clean the floor.

### MONTHLY

- Vacuum details.
- Empty & clean the shredder.
- Clean window treatments.
- Wipe wall & trim smudges.

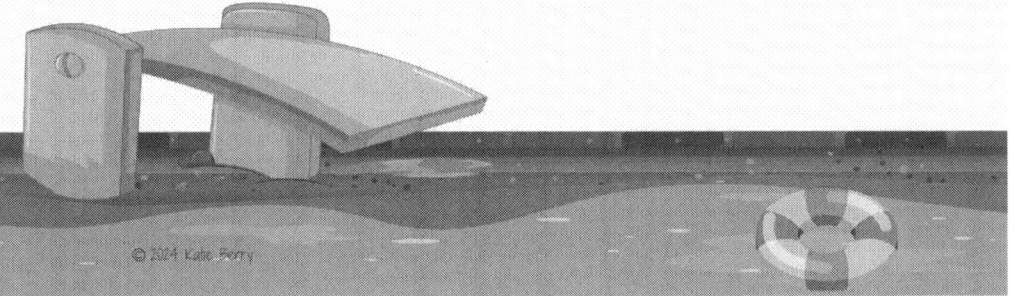

© 2024 Katie Berry

## Part Five
# RESEARCH LAB

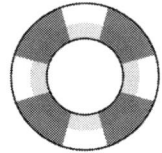

### WARNING

You are about to enter the Research Lab. Labs are about experimenting, which means your first attempts may not be 100% perfect. That's the entire point: try things, test to see if they work, and revise your experiment based on what you learn.

Like all labs, this one starts with an observation: you want a cleaner home. It asks a question: how do you get there? What happens next is where things can start going wrong. Don't try to repeat my routine and expect it to perfectly work in your home. You need to experiment and adjust until you find the perfect result for you.

Then don't quit!

*Chapter Twenty*
## MY WEEKLY ROUTINE

*I*f you scanned the Table of Contents and jumped ahead to this section, go back to the beginning and start there. I put this toward the end *for a reason*!

And if you ignored what I just said, then maybe you should head straight to the section about self-sabotage because I'm not kidding. This will seem overwhelming until you understand the process involved.

Listen, I understand why you might want to just get to the good stuff. When we're swamped, we just want to get the job done. We think the fix is like a recipe: add this much of cleaning, that much of vacuuming, fold in the laundry, stir in some extra attention at the end and voilà: a home that is not just clean but will stay that way, too!

I'm sorry to be the one to tell you, but it doesn't work like that. Without understanding *why* each step matters, we sabotage our success by changing it.

It's like changing a recipe without understanding how the ingredients work. Let's say you're used to substituting applesauce for oil when baking to reduce calories. If you try that with a croissant recipe, it will never work. Without bits of fat melting, you won't get the air pockets which produce the flaky results that makes croissants so good. Haphazardly changing the recipe doomed the results.

Randomly changing things around can doom cleaning, too. For example, some cleaning methods apply to one surface but not another. Take steel wool, for instance: it works brilliantly on cast iron pans before reseasoning them, but if you use it on a stainless steel set even reseasoning won't fix the damage.

It applies to cleaning routines as well. If you don't understand how the habit chains and daily resets work, or why doing them every day is important, you may never break out of the binge-cleaning cycle.

My system works for *my* home. Until you understand what's involved and why, you won't know how to make it work for *your* home.

But if you just want the answer, here it is: build the habit of consistent cleaning. *Ta dah!* Do you feel equipped to do it now? Of course not! You already know it's the solution, that's why you bought the book. It's the how-to part you're here for and that happens in the pages before now.

I want you to succeed. So please, don't sabotage your success: go back to page 1 and read from the beginning. Then you can tweak the recipe to suit yourself while still getting the same delicious results.

*Without understanding why each step matters, we sabotage our success by changing it.*

# CLEANING 101

## DAILY TIDYING

I have never jumped out of bed excited to clean my home. Not one single time. In fact, when my kids were younger and my husband's chemo for brain cancer caused him to vomit unexpectedly (and profusely), just knowing I had to clean made me want to stay in bed. For*ever*.

But I function best when my surroundings are tidy. A cluttered mess makes me anxious, and then I can't be creative. Since creative expression is vital to my happiness, I clean to create an environment in which I am at my best.

Years of practice has taught me that the fastest, easiest way to make that happen is through daily resets and consistent weekly cleaning. I make both of those easier by intentionally picking up after myself.

*I clean to create an environment in which I am at my best.*

That doesn't mean I enjoy it. So, I clean in small bursts throughout the day:

- Daily kitchen tasks while I'm waiting on my coffee pot to work its magic.
- Daily bathroom tasks after I'm dressed for the day.
- Daily bedroom tasks before work.
- Then, as I head to bed, I tidy the living room.

Sounds like a lot? It felt that way, until I made it non-negotiable. When I no longer had to decide if I felt like cleaning and just did it instead, cleaning took up less of my mental energy. I stopped spending time talking myself into it, figuring out ways to put it off, and working myself up to it.

When I started just doing it day after day, consistently, cleaning went from being a mountain to a molehill. It began taking less time, too.

## MY WEEKLY CLEANING ROUTINE

I use a room-based approach which means I clean one room each weekday. Most take 15-20 minutes, depending on the monthly add-on chore. I prefer cleaning right after work to get it out of the way, but if something comes up I'll do it immediately after dinner. *Period.*

My laundry routine syncs with the cleaning, so I'm not building Mount Laundry all week then spending Saturday conquering it. I much prefer weekends filled with fun, don't you?

So, here's what my weekdays look like:

- **Monday:** Clean the kitchen. Wash kitchen linens and rugs.
- **Tuesday:** Clean the bathrooms. Wash bath linens and mats.
- **Wednesday:** Clean the bedrooms. Wash bedding.
- **Thursday:** Clean the living room and family room. Wash the throw blankets and another round of bath towels.
- **Friday:** Clean the entryway and my home office. Wash clothes.

*Most rooms take 15-20 minutes, depending on the monthly add-on chore — as long as I'm consistent about the daily tidying.*

## CLEANING 101

Now, as I've mentioned, I don't ask myself if I feel like it: it's on my schedule, so I get it done. It doesn't matter if the room already looks tidy: in fact, that's even better because then cleaning only takes minutes!

Because if there's one thing I know about me and cleaning my home, the instant I start debating whether I should or not, I won't. (Thanks, ADHD.)

## Chapter Twenty-One
# HOW I MANAGE IT WITH ADHD

*I*'ve always known *how* to clean things properly—my mother taught me that growing up, and not always calmly. But knowing how to clean a countertop isn't the same as knowing how to clean an entire kitchen, let alone how often.

Putting that together into a routine for all the rooms in my home was a challenge, especially with my ADHD. Transitioning from an attorney with a support staff to being a stay-at-home mom was a struggle.

In the office, I had a secretary who kept me on track. Deadlines, appointments, and signatures were necessary parts of my job, and she made sure I did them. If I'd ever told her I didn't feel like meeting a client or signing a petition, she would have laughed. Those tasks had to be done regardless of my mood or motivation.

I had to take the same approach at home. Whether I feel like it or not isn't up for discussion, because I know I function best when my home is clean.

It's not being mean to myself to care for my environment; it's being kind to myself in the long run. One way feels good for a while but eventually makes me feel anxious because I'm

## CLEANING 101

surrounded by a mess. The other provides long-term stress relief and comfort. I also eat vegetables and brush my teeth without thinking of it as being mean to myself. Don't you?

*Sometimes, you may just need some tough self-love.*

I share this because whenever I talk about using routines to manage my ADHD and keep my home clean, someone tells me *their* ADHD means they can't remember a routine, much less follow one. My response is always the same: can you drive?

If you learned to drive, it's because you practiced until you could keep track of all the different inputs: speed, street names, turns, and other cars. You memorized routes. So if you can drive, you can learn to do things with enough practice, visual cues, and patience.

Sometimes, you may just need some tough self-love. I know, yuck. *Cleaning is boring!* But if you want a clean home, you either need to learn how to overcome your obstacles or find someone to clean it for you.

But let's be clear: not everyone with ADHD can drive. Whether it's attention deficit, executive dysfunction, time-blindness, or impulse management, some of us simply *can't*. That's just how we're wired, and no one should feel shamed over something beyond their control. That's what family is for.

## Chapter Twenty-Two
# GETTING THE FAMILY INVOLVED

Before we got married, my husband kept a tidy home, did his own laundry, cooked his own meals, and washed his own dishes.

I, on the other hand, worked two jobs to pay my way through college and walked everywhere because I still couldn't afford a car. The only reason my apartment stayed tidy was because I was rarely there, and I didn't own much.

A strange thing happened in our first months of newlywed bliss: we swapped roles almost entirely. I'd bought into all the cultural messages which said good wives keep clean homes, cook meals from scratch, and stay on top of the laundry. Meanwhile, he bought into their counterparts which said that men make money, squash bugs, and fix things.

Parenthood reinforced these messages, and I grew increasingly furious that the pressure of being "a good mom" felt like nonstop work while being "a good dad" looked an awful lot like nonstop playtime.

Now, listen, I'm not trying to win you over to thinking the traditional gender roles need updating. I'm simply trying to explain that I'd spent years stressed out because I'd defined my worth by how clean my home was. If our home was spotless, it proved I was a good wife and mother. If it was messy, it meant I'd failed.

> *I'd spent years stressed out because I'd defined my worth by how clean my home was.*

Messes also left me feeling like my family disrespected my time and effort. It seemed like they didn't care if others looked down on me if our home wasn't constantly clean. Because, let's face it, most people still judge women more harshly for a messy home than they judge a man or the older kids who also live there. It's not fair, but it is what it is. For now.

A home is a family community, and by definition, communities are group projects. Unfortunately, I'd taught my family to think of me as the Cleaning Fairy. What I hadn't taught them was to participate in the most important community they'll ever be part of: their home.

Everything about life got better once I did.

## HABIT CHAINS FOR THE WHOLE FAMILY

Habit chains are basically the things we all try to teach our kids.

- Done with that toy? Put it away before getting a new one.
- Getting home from school? Put your shoes in the cabinet and hang up your backpack.

- Changing clothes? Put the dirty ones in the laundry sorter.
- Done bathing? Hang up your towel.
- Done brushing teeth? Rinse your sink.
- Leaving the room? Put things away.
- Had a snack? Wash your dish or put it in the dishwasher.
- Borrowing the car? Get your fast-food wrappers out of it. (And fill the tank while you're at it, kid.)
- Going to bed? Take your stuff.

Of course, when I decided to go from doing everything for my family to getting my kids to pick up after themselves, all I had to do was suggest it over dinner.

They listened intently and munched on the freshly baked homemade bread slathered in hand-churned butter. Then they smiled sweetly, wiped their little mouths with the cloth napkins I'd woven out of unicorn hair said, "Yes, Mother, we will adopt these habit chains to keep our home clean, so you don't have to pick up after us anymore. Huzzah!"

I'm kidding. That absolutely did not happen. *None of it.*

What happened was exactly what anyone should expect when they tell their family they're all going to start cleaning up after themselves from that moment forward: they rolled their eyes and ignored me. The oldest snorted. The youngest one laughed.

See, in the past, I'd tried chore charts with cute little stickers, cleaning games with fun prizes, pleading, yelling, and bribery with exorbitant allowances. None of it worked. They knew it, I knew it, and I'm pretty sure the family dog knew it, too.

Now, of course, I can look back and see how my then-undiagnosed ADHD *might've* affected whether I followed through on any of these things. But we were all younger and less knowledgeable then.

So, that's what I started with: follow-through. And I did it by focusing on building *my* habit chains. Day after day, I picked up after myself, cleaned small messes as I discovered them, and consistently cleaned one room a day. I didn't involve them. I don't recall even telling them what I was doing.

But after about a month, I began noticing that the only things out of place was *their* stuff. I'd learned to consistently put mine away. I'd learned habit chains, I'd been modeling them, and now that my messes weren't hiding theirs, it was time to help them learn habit chains, too.

My kids have the same selective hearing that all kids seem to have. You can tell them to do (or not do) something, and while making eye contact, they'll nod and say they understand. You can even have them repeat it back to you perfectly, promising to do (or not do) it. Then, they will immediately forget. When you call them on it, they will flat-out deny that you ever told them anything.

Since they were both experts at forgetting anything I said, my little gaslighting geniuses needed help remembering things. So, I resorted to the one parental tactic that any kid remembers: I intentionally annoyed them.

From that day forward, if I found their stuff sitting out, I'd cheerfully interrupt what they were doing and walk with them through the process of carrying out the habit. For example, when my son dumped his school bag on the kitchen floor, I interrupted his gaming, walked with him to find the backpack, and had him take it to the hook in the entryway where it belonged. The next day, I had to interrupt him on the phone to repeat it. The third day, I had to stop him mid-snack. On the fourth day, he didn't need me.

Annoying? Sure, but I hadn't nagged or raised my voice, which would have given him a reason to get upset. I'd just inconvenienced him enough to make putting his school bag away more appealing than leaving it out.

*I resorted to the one parental tactic that any kid remembers: I intentionally annoyed them.*

We went through the exact same routine with plates he'd leave in the sink, game controllers on the coffee table, and dirty socks all over the house. After that, he realized it was just easier to put things away.

With my daughter, who'd come home and shower after practice, the issue was wet towels and sweaty clothes left on the bathroom floor. Interrupting a girl in the middle of a group phone call about some drama at school is *not* a fun experience, but with much muttering and eye-rolls, she did pick them up.

The next day, when it happened again, I thought being more playful by singing my request in a false operatic voice would help avoid the loud stomping and door-slamming. I thought wrong. But there wasn't a third day, so that's something.

See, my kids are smart, just like yours. It didn't take them long to realize I was starting to enjoy the challenge of coming up with ways to be annoying. Other times I wore a mullet wig, used a megaphone, or tap danced through the room where they were watching TV. Once when I was ignored, I got frustrated and shut off all the electricity to the house at the main fuse box.

(Please remember this is not a parenting book, and I have never claimed to be Mother of the Year material.)

But it didn't take them long to realize they were in control of the solution: put their things away, and I'd have no reason to be a dork.

Fortunately, they chose wisely.

Sure, there were lapses. But once the habits had set, I just had to say, "Do you know where your backpack is?" or "Pretty sure I saw a towel on the bathroom floor." They'd take care of it quickly

## CLEANING 101

rather than have their mother dig out that mullet wig which, frankly, looked awesome.

*It didn't take them long to realize they were in control of the solution: put their things away.*

Within a few weeks, our home was consistently tidier. I spent less time cleaning, and they figured out their chores didn't take as long either. We all had more time to do the things we enjoyed, so we got along better, too. Yes, even when they were teens!

This change didn't happen overnight. As I've said, consistent cleaning habits develop through effort and repetition. It's not something you do once and then forget, it's a process.

And speaking of the process, let's get you started adopting the system to suit your own home.

## Chapter Twenty-Three
# TAKE THE PLUNGE

With the 12-week plan that follows, you slowly replace your current system one habit chain at a time. If you haven't been following any approach until now, that's okay too. Just try to keep things clean enough that the Health Department doesn't need to stop by while you're learning new routines.

Then keep going. Make it a daily habit to tidy up after yourself and teach your family to do the same. Keep cleaning supplies handy, simplify storage, cut down on clutter, and clean on a consistent schedule to prevent things from becoming overwhelming.

And if life does become overwhelming and you need to step away from your routine, give yourself permission to do so. Sometimes, you need to rest and recharge.

*Even if you've tried and quit in the past, it is never too late to start again.*

I learned this lesson the hard way while writing this book when

# CLEANING 101

I ignored a mild case of swimmer's ear. I was afraid taking a break would disrupt my routine, but all it did was make the problem worse and prolong my recovery. Lucky for both of us, taking that time off to recuperate allowed me to finish writing this book. I was back to swimming before wrapping up the second draft.

See, resting is not the same as quitting. You can and should feel *good* about resting when you need it: you're taking care of more than just your body when you do. Ease back into it when you're ready. Even if you've tried and quit in the past, it is never too late to start again.

*That* is why I've bored you with all the swimming stuff, so you understand that you can do hard things, even if they seem overwhelming at first. Commitment and consistency will help you see progress where you once struggled.

But like getting back into the swim of things, it's easier to stay consistent if you work up to it. Do it methodically. Don't push yourself. Then, you won't need to worry about drowning in mess because you'll have built a buoy that keeps you afloat. Your habit chains will anchor the daily tidying that resets your space, and weekly cleaning will take care of what's left.

Stick with it, and you'll create a space where you can be the best version of *you*.

*Just keep swimming,*
*xo Katie*

# 12-Week Foundational Plan

| | Practice Habit Chains | Daily Tidying | Weekly Cleaning | Monthly Tasks |
|---|---|---|---|---|
| Week 1 | Read the book | Your usual routine. | Your usual routine. | |
| Week 2 | Kitchen | All rooms | Your usual routine. | |
| Week 3 | Kitchen, living spaces | All rooms | Kitchen | |
| Week 4 | Kitchen, living spaces, bedrooms | All rooms | Kitchen, living spaces | |
| Week 5 | Kitchen, living spaces, bedrooms, bathrooms | All rooms | Kitchen, living spaces, bedrooms | |
| Week 6 | Kitchen, living spaces, bedrooms, bathrooms | All rooms | Kitchen, living spaces, bedrooms, bathrooms | |

© 2024 Katie Berry

# 12-Week Foundational Plan

| | Practice Habit Chains | Daily Tidying | Weekly Cleaning | Monthly Tasks |
|---|---|---|---|---|
| Week 7 | Kitchen, living spaces, bedrooms, bathrooms | All rooms | Kitchen, living spaces, bedrooms, bathrooms | Kitchen |
| Week 8 | Kitchen, living spaces, bedrooms, bathrooms, entryway | All rooms | Kitchen, living spaces, bedrooms, bathrooms | Kitchen, living spaces |
| Week 9 | Kitchen, living spaces, bedrooms, bathrooms, entryway | All rooms | Kitchen, living spaces, bedrooms, bathrooms, entryway | Kitchen, living spaces, bedrooms |
| Week 10 | Kitchen, living spaces, bedrooms, bathrooms, entryway, office | All rooms | Kitchen, living spaces, bedrooms, bathrooms, entryway | Kitchen, living spaces, bedrooms, bathrooms |
| Week 11 | All | All rooms | Kitchen, living spaces, bedrooms, bathrooms, entryway, office | Kitchen, living spaces, bedrooms, bathrooms, entryway |
| Week 12 | All | All rooms | All rooms | All rooms |

© 2024 Katie Berry

## ALSO BY KATIE BERRY

30 Days to a Clean and Organized House

Cleaning on YOUR Schedule

And visit the author's website at HousewifeHowTos.com

Printed in Great Britain
by Amazon

49849272R00077